Robin Ward's Heritage West Coast

Robin Ward's

Harbour Publishing

Heritage West Coast

Copyright © 1993 by Robin Ward

Harbour Publishing Co. Ltd.
P.O. Box 219
Madeira Park, BC
Canada V0N 2H0

Designed by Robin Ward
Typeset in Baskerville
Printed and bound in Canada

Canadian Cataloguing in Publication Data

Ward, Robin, 1950–
 Robin Ward's heritage West Coast

 ISBN 1-55017-095-3

 1. Historic buildings — British Columbia — Pacific Coast.
2. Historic buildings — Washington (State) — Pacific Coast.
3. Pacific Coast (B.C.) — Description and travel.   4. Pacific
Coast (Wash.) — Description and travel.
I. Title. II. Title: Heritage West Coast
FC3812.W37 1993   971.1   C93-091646-8
F1087.8.W37 1993

CONTENTS *

* Vancouver locations, unless noted

Contents

Acknowledgements

With thanks to my wife, Porta, for her help and encouragement; my editor, Mary Schendlinger; the Vancouver Sun; the City of Vancouver Heritage Planning Department; Heritage Vancouver; the Empress Hotel, Victoria; and the many people and institutions who, directly and indirectly, assisted in the compilation of this book.

INTRODUCTION

When Harbour Publishing invited me to produce a second book of drawings and commentary based on my weekly column in the *Vancouver Sun*, I wondered if I had enough material to work with. The first book, *Robin Ward's Vancouver*, explored Vancouver and its history through the city's architecture, and featured many of the city's better-known heritage buildings. In this new collection of drawings and text, I have ventured further afield: to Seattle, a city that, in its history and architecture, is comparable but also a contrast to Vancouver; to Victoria, which is quite different from both its larger neighbours; and to Vancouver's periphery.

When I moved to Vancouver from Europe and began writing for the *Sun*, I began to explore my new surroundings by walking the city's streets and sketching its buildings. I know no better way to feel the pulse of a city than to stand on street corners or in doorways drawing for hours. While much of my research is done in public libraries, city archives, at City Hall planning departments, and by talking to architects and developers, often the most lucid, entertaining and heartfelt accounts of local urban history come from the proverbial man in the street. People politely interrupt me when I'm drawing to tell me: "That was a strange old house, we used to play hide-and-seek in the garden—we thought the house was haunted," or that "Gran used to live there" and how the district has changed. Others have memories of urban working days, of streetcars and streets full of people, and neoclassical banks and office buildings with "plush elevators, all polished wood panelling, and an operator to open and close the doors!"

Listening to these comments and reading the letters I receive at the *Sun*, I am encouraged by how often and how strongly residents express interest in and concern for their surroundings. Their stories bear out the fact, not always understood by developers or city bureaucrats, that as well as displaying pleasurable and sometimes ebullient decoration, old buildings give meaning, memory and continuity to city life. As a result, in the course of writing the column in the *Sun* I have been motivated to tackle contemporary debate about architecture, preservation and development, and to comment on government and public response—particularly in Vancouver and Victoria—to these issues, and the increasing economic pressure for change affecting heritage buildings and their preservation.

As in the first book, many of Vancouver's notable old buildings are included here, but with a greater emphasis than before on residential architecture. Development and preservation issues that affect city centre heritage buildings—the replacement of the Georgia Medical–Dental building by Cathedral Place in Vancouver, and the development of the Eaton Centre in Victoria, for example—receive their fair share of publicity and are featured here. But in residential neighbourhoods, particularly older estates, demolition and redevelopment of perfectly good homes continues without much debate beyond the areas affected. This process has a more pervasive effect than individual losses downtown. It engenders a sense, striking at the heart of community life, that change is not always for the best — many people know that bulldozing elegant old houses and charming cottages for jerry-built monster homes is an affront to architectural standards and visually damaging to traditional neighbourhoods.

This sense of loss, of being at sea in an relentless swell of change, was poignantly expressed by a Vancouver reader of my column who wrote, "Almost all of the original houses on our block have been demolished in the past few years, along with their beautiful old gardens, to be replaced with monstrous houses squeezed onto thirty-three-foot lots. Our little house is now dwarfed by its massive new neighbours. Nowadays the old houses haven't a chance. Land is at a premium, and the people who can afford to live here want brand new, big homes." Even Shaughnessy Heights, Vancouver's finest Edwardian residential estate, is threatened by builders who buy heritage homes and demolish them to substitute profitable but cheap imitations, thereby eroding the area's heritage character and prestige — the very qualities which make Shaughnessy such a desirable address. Without firm intervention by the city, which currently applies only some rather vapid design guidelines to

ensure that new homes "fit in," Shaughnessy could soon become a mock-Tudor parody of its former self.

In many other cities, districts of such architectural quality — both residential and commercial — are designated "conservation areas" with strict rules as to form, detailing, and quality and type of materials employed. Buildings in and around conservation areas qualify for grant aid to help with restoration and maintenance, and tax breaks promote and reward heritage preservation. Where conservation is practised, most people accept its overall benefit to the neighbourhood and the city, and gradually a climate is created in which heritage preservation of more than just individual monuments is seen to be a positive social force.

In Vancouver, for all its sophistication, the city's boosters and builders still haven't quite shrugged off their laissez-faire, boom-and-bust frontier mentality. This is part of the city's character and heritage too. But it militates against heritage planners' ability to convince politicians, owners and developers that heritage homes and commercial buildings should be retained. Even buildings and artifacts that have received city heritage designation can, as the case of the Canadian National railway station sign shows, be at the mercy of expediency and council whim. Also emanating from City Hall are modern building codes applied rigidly to old buildings when any change of use — frequently necessary to make restoration possible financially — is to be made. Complying is often a daunting, time-consuming and expensive process. The building owner may recover the cost through the higher property value of a restored building, but will also be hit with higher taxes.

As for the city's so-called "heritage foundation," to be endowed to "promote and encourage public interest in [Vancouver's] built heritage" and "to fund, support preservation, conservation, and maintenance efforts by citizens," little has been heard of it since it was launched two years ago. Sufficient public funding to kick-start the program was not forthcoming — an indication of Vancouver's ambivalent attitude toward its architectural heritage, and of City Hall's traditional reluctance to spend public money, or to take any action to preserve old buildings that interferes with free enterprise and private property rights.

It is significant that three of the city's major and most admired heritage restoration and infill projects — Granville Island, the Sinclair Centre and the Four Sisters Housing Cooperative — were funded largely by federal and provincial agencies, rather than municipal ones. It is the province that has been responsible for the conservation areas that do exist in Vancouver, namely Chinatown and Gastown, and for designating several of the city's most prominent buildings. There is still no legislation in Vancouver, where it is most needed, to protect the city's architectural heritage from redevelopment and the excesses of the free market.

Fortunately, things are changing in Vancouver. There have been preservation successes, Yaletown for example, and designations of buildings and city initiatives in compiling and updating its heritage inventory. Council also recently passed a more liberal heritage density transfer policy, specifically to encourage the retention of heritage buildings: basically it allows owners to transfer unused density — extra floors of height, for example, allowable by the zoning in the area concerned — to other parts of the inner city, rather than to an adjacent site. And there is an awareness gradually percolating among officials that preservation is a desirable course to take. In 1990, for example, Vancouver City Council approved planners' recommendations for Victory Square, which is one of Canada's best preserved Edwardian commercial areas, but which has long been neglected and is currently dilapidated. Council members established a potentially successful policy to retain existing buildings, and to ensure sympathetically scaled new construction. Most significant, however, is the growing individual and community awareness in Vancouver that heritage matters, and that in the future, citizens' voices will be heard.

ROBIN WARD
Vancouver BC
August 1993

Glen Brae, an extraordinary composition topped with a pair of voluptuous domes, is the most memorable mansion on Vancouver's Shaughnessy Heights. There's nothing sedate or elegant about this eccentric villa, completed in 1910 at 1690 Matthews Avenue. Restraint was clearly not a word in the vocabulary of William Tait, the owner, or architects Parr & Fee whose trademarks were gutsy cornices on the commercial buildings and turrets on the houses they designed.

Tait, a lumber and property baron, wanted the house to remind him of his native Scotland and he briefed his architects accordingly. Parr & Fee responded with their idea of what a Scottish baronial home should look like. The result is a flamboyant exercise in nostalgia — an Edwardian display of capitalist gain buying into the romance of aristocracy. From its Corinthian-columned entrance canopy to a ballroom said to have been laid on seaweed to add spring to the polka, Glen Brae is the epitome of Belle Epoque extravagance.

Other features of the home include glazed brickwork, rusticated stonework and Art Nouveau stained glass on the window arcades below the domes. The house is set in a formally planted garden defined by a superb cast iron fence with pillared gateways. The fence and gateways were manufactured in Scotland by Walter Macfarlane and Company and cast at the Saracen Foundry in Glasgow. Macfarlane's company exported cast iron railings, bandstands and even complete buildings to every corner of the British Empire in Victorian and Edwardian times. Glen Brae's florid ironwork, a rare example in Canada, gives the house added distinction and convincing period character.

Dreams of the "emerald isle" inspired this home, historically one of the most significant in Vancouver. It was built for the aristocratically titled Right Honourable Baron Shaughnessy of Montreal, Canada and Ashford, County Limerick, Ireland. The house, at 1551 Angus Drive, was one of the first homes built on Shaughnessy Heights, the exclusive Edwardian residential enclave developed by the Canadian Pacific Railway across False Creek from the city centre.

Shaughnessy, after whom Shaughnessy Heights was named, was president of the CPR from 1899 to 1918, and he established himself on his estate by commissioning a German builder, C. S. Shindler, to design this "Irish hunting lodge" as his Vancouver *pied-a-terre*. Shaughnessy already had a grand home in Montreal, a Second Empire-style mansion built in 1874, which still stands, having been rescued from dereliction as the centrepiece of the Canadian Centre for Architecture.

This Vancouver house, quaintly described on Shindler's blueprints as a "Cottage for Sir Thomas Shaughnessy," was completed in 1910 in a country manor style showing, in its low-slung gables, the lingering influence of the Arts and Crafts movement of nineteenth-century England. In 1919 the house was sold to C. W. Frazee of the Royal Bank, whose family have since maintained its character. Relatively modest by Shaughnessy standards, but set in a large picturesque garden, the house has mellowed with age — unlike some over-restored Shaughnessy dwellings whose patina has been removed — and remains in almost original condition.

When Robert Dunsmuir hired architects Warren H. Williams and Arthur L. Smith of Portland, Oregon to design Craigdarroch Castle, completed in 1889 on the highest point above Victoria, they responded with an extravagant pile of whimsy designed to recall the baronial architecture of their client's native land.

Robert Dunsmuir was a small-town Ayrshire coal mine manager who left Scotland in 1850 on a three-year contract with the Hudson's Bay Company to prospect for coal on Vancouver Island. When his contract expired he turned entrepreneur. By hard work, cool, flinty character and good fortune, he became the wealthiest, if not always the most popular, man in the province, capping his career with a seat in the provincial legislature. At its height, the Dunsmuir industrial empire included coal mines, railways, steamships, iron works, sawmills, a quarry, and press and property investments.

Craigdarroch's architects, like Glen Brae's in Vancouver, designed what they thought a Scottish baronial home should look like. They certainly captured the moody romanticism of the time. Craigdarroch looks as if it has leapt off the pages of a novel by Sir Walter Scott. While "Scottish baronial" broadly describes the spirit of the place, Scotch broth might best describe the home's eclectic mixture of styles. The pointed, corbelled turrets are distinctly Scottish baronial in style, but were originally characteristic of the Loire chateaux of sixteenth-century France (as is Craigdarroch's chateau-style slate roof). The decorative ironwork on the balconies is a typically Victorian embellishment. The rusticated stonework and arched windows show the influence of Richardsonian Romanesque, a style popular in America at the time, while the irregular tall chimneys hark back to Tudor England. There's even a hint of Renaissance Italy, as much as there is of contemporary North American fashion, in the columned porch that extends halfway around the home as a loggia.

Lest the exterior leaves you in doubt, beyond Craigdarroch Castle's porte-cochere and the softly filtered light of its cramped vestibule, the hallway firmly establishes the mansion's baronial pretension. The hall could be in a Scottish hunting lodge: stone fireplace, bronze bas-relief highland scene, and trophies (stag and ram's heads) mounted on the wood-panelled walls. The extensive sitting room is lavishly decorated in Regency style. The library, suitably wood-panelled and illuminated by Tiffany-style stained glass showing Scottish bluebells, thistles and hollyberries, is dominated by a massive carved fireplace bearing the epigram "Reading Maketh the Full Man"—very Victorian in its righteousness. There's a fireside epigram in the hallway too, more cloying than righteous, but no less Victorian. "Welcome ever smiles and Farewell goes out sighing," it sentimentally proclaims.

There's also a modern notice in the hall that advises visitors to "look up." The sight is quite astonishing—a spectacular stairwell rising through four storeys to the full height of the building, with nooks on the landings to sit and catch your breath as you climb. Every surface you pass during this giddy ascent is covered in what appears to be hand-carved wood panelling. But it turns out, like all of Craigdarroch's wild baronial conceit, to be an enjoyable, expensive sham. The wood panelling was manufactured by Andrews and Company of Chicago, which from 1885 to 1895 employed 500 men in four factories where "elaborate machines churned out acres of fine panelling and marque-

try flooring." These were dispatched across the continent in railway boxcars to glorify offices, churches and homes.

Craigdarroch, for all its fine carving and craftsmanship beyond the panelled stairs is, in this evocation of aristocratic life, the quintessential Victorian capitalist's fantasy—a mail order ancestral home.

Robert Dunsmuir died shortly before Craigdarroch was completed, and his wife Joan lived in the house until her death in 1908. (It is her brooding presence that permeates the gloomy abode today.) The contents were sold at a spectacular auction in 1909. The house changed hands over the years until efforts by the Craigdarroch Castle Historical Museum Society and the City of Victoria secured its future as a heritage site. The society has worked hard to restore the home and to keep it open to the public.

Outside Victoria, just west of Esquimalt, there is another Dunsmuir castle—Hatley Park, begun in 1908 for James Dunsmuir, Robert and Joan's eldest son. Hatley Park (now Royal Roads Military College), set on an 800-acre estate, is even grander than Craigdarroch. James Dunsmuir succeeded his father as president of the family firm, and later became Premier and Lieutenant Governor of British Columbia. His taste for the high life at Government House led him to commission architect Samuel Maclure to design this castellated stately home in elaborate sixteenth-century English style, complete with a lofty Gothic Revival entrance hall. The extensive estate, where Dunsmuir retired to live like feudal potentate, included Italianate and Japanese gardens (well preserved), a model farm, dwellings for a troop of Chinese labourers, a conservatory for exotic plants and mooring for his 218-foot Clydebuilt steam yacht.

This twenty-two-room manor house at 3875 Point Grey
Road in Vancouver was designed by the firm Maclure &
Fox and built in 1913. Samuel Maclure was Victoria's best
known residential architect at the time. His many homes
for the local *crème de la crème* (or those who wished to be considered so) include his first major Vancouver commission,
Gabriola, built in 1901 for sugar king B. T. Rogers. Following the success of the Rogers mansion, Maclure opened
an office in Vancouver and sent his colleague, English architect Cecil Crocker Fox, over from Victoria to run it.
Maclure & Fox built several expansive Tudor Revival
homes for wealthy clients in Vancouver while maintaining
a more varied output in Victoria.

Most Maclure & Fox houses in Vancouver were built on
Shaughnessy Heights and can only be viewed from the
street. But Brock House, once owned by the RCMP (showing a taste for establishment privilege) is now a city-owned
property, open to the public. The Brock House Society restored it in the mid-1970s as a social and cultural centre for
senior citizens. Here you can sense Edwardian high society
at play behind the half-timbered exterior, and on the shore-
line grounds where garden party guests would admire the
view across English Bay to the North Shore mountains
beyond.

In 1909, Vancouver business boosters strung a banner across Hastings Street which declared: *Many men making money means much for Vancouver* — an ethos which still informs political and corporate life in the city and which places a low premium on heritage conservation. To the ill-informed, heritage preservation is seen as being neither financially nor socially rewarding. Ironically, many of the heritage buildings which have been preserved in Vancouver are the former residences of the rich and famous. Vancouver boomed in the Edwardian era, and those who benefited chose to express their wealth in lavish pseudo-Baronial and mock-Tudor homes.

E. P. Davis, a corporate lawyer, commissioned one of the finest of these dwellings from architects Maclure & Fox and sited it on virgin property on Point Grey, overlooking the anchorage where Captain George Vancouver exchanged greetings with the Spanish navigators Galiano and Valdes in 1792. The property, now part of the University of British Columbia's campus, was quite remote from the city when the Davis home was built in 1911–12.

Now restored, Cecil Green Park (named after the alumnus who saved the house and donated it to the university) shows Maclure & Fox at their picturesque best. The interior with its wood panelling, leaded glass, lofty foyer and, in one columned lounge, delicate neoclassical plasterwork, is an enchanting sequence of spaces. Outside, the rambling residence is a riot of dormers, stone chimneys and half-timbering set in a verdant clifftop Edwardian garden.

Built on the highest point of Vancouver Heights, which rise steeply southeast of the Second Narrows bridge and the city's industrial waterfront, Overlynn is Burnaby's finest heritage home. The house, which is relatively unknown, was completed in 1909 for Scottish tea importer and wholesaler Charles J. Peter, who promoted development on Vancouver Heights. Peter visualized a Shaughnessy-type estate for which his own house, at 3755 McGill Street, would set the tone. But the city's well-to-do found Shaughnessy a cleaner and more convenient location, despite Vancouver Heights' spectacular views across the city and to Lynn Valley (hence the name of the house) in the mountains on the North Shore.

Architects Maclure & Fox were commissioned to design the house in the Tudor Revival style for which they were well known. Wood panelling and stained glass are well preserved inside. Outside, rough-cut granite on the ground floor surmounted by half-timbering, wide eaves, hipped roof and prominent stone chimneys combine in a composition of quiet distinction, in keeping with the popular image of British landed gentry to which colonial businessmen of the time aspired.

In 1936 the house became a convent and girls' school, Seton Academy. Regrettably, a delightful conservatory abutting the south wing of the house was demolished and replaced by a half-timbered Gothic Revival chapel. The property was further altered after 1970 when it was bought by a seniors' housing society which built an eighteen-storey tower in the garden. Nevertheless, the house and part of the original garden are still well preserved.

The modest to medium-size homes built on large lots across Vancouver's west side in the first half of this century form a stylistically varied, but generally consistent suburban environment. The homes were built to the same scale and aligned to face their tree-lined streets side by side so that none would claim too much attention. Those that did attempt to upstage their neighbours did so by architectural style, humour and whimsy. Good manners were the order of the day.

The same cannot be said for today's pretentiously over-scaled "monster homes" whose proliferation on the west side (and elsewhere in the city) is remorselessly eroding the character of traditional streetscapes and neighbourhoods. The monster homes seem to be designed on the premise that every family needs half a dozen bathrooms and a two-storey atrium in the hall. The exterior style of these bloated buildings, often pedimented and porticoed, veers toward classicism but without the refinement one might expect. Their builders and buyers appear to know nothing of the architecture of ancient Greece or Rome.

The designers of older west side homes also raided the history books but treated their sources with more respect and understanding than is generally shown today — and they had the luxury of affordable and readily available craftsmanship. Local builders offered everything from Spanish Colonial and mock-Tudor to neo-Georgian and French chateau styles copied from grander, architect-designed Shaughnessy homes or published pattern book plans.

Some of these homes are delightfully odd and fanciful. The cozy Cotswold cottage (below) at 587 West King Edward Avenue, built by builder B. T. Lea in 1941 with steam-heated shingles imitating thatched roofing, should really be in Disneyland — it's already something of a tourist attraction. If you didn't want a cottage your real estate agent might have suggested a castle, like this miniature Norman chateau (left) at 3825 West 39th Avenue. This house and a similar doll's house chateau next door, both built in 1938 by a builder, J. S. Wood, anchor an exceptionally well-preserved period streetscape — so far, not a monster home in sight.

The Haigler House, at 3537 West 30th Avenue in Vancouver, was built for merchant George Haigler and completed in 1925. Haigler was friendly with ships' captains and it is rumoured that some of the granite used on the house came in ballast from Scotland, on vessels calling in Vancouver for cargoes of lumber. Haigler's interest in the sea and maritime trade was echoed in the wood-panelled rooms inside the house where bronze light fittings were decorated with sailing ships.

Local stonemason Duncan McLean hand-cut the hexagonal granite facing and installed a matching granite fireplace inside. Even the garden wall and foundations use this material, some of which McLean cut from boulders gathered on then surrounding vacant lots. The wide, single-beamed porch with its twin stubby columns, low-pitched gabled roof, overhanging eaves and protruding brackets, rough-cut stone, and overall handmade quality are typical of the Craftsman style of domestic architecture which was popular in Vancouver from around 1910 through to the 1920s.

Craftsman style dwellings are, typically, bungalows, although some expand to quite dizzying proportions. The style originated in California around the turn of the century and its semi-rural picturesque effect and use of natural materials made such homes singularly appropriate on the West Coast. Other influences can be discerned. The Arts and Crafts movement from England, with its utopian em-phasis on traditional regional domestic architecture, finely crafted furnishings and fittings, and a certain Japanese influence — both current in late nineteenth-century Europe and North America — are evident in the more sophisticated examples of the style. Most Craftsman homes, however, were copied by local builders from magazine articles and other published sources.

The Haigler House was one of the best in Vancouver, particularly because it was, until 1991, set in an enchanting garden. There were once 35 species of trees, 56 types of shrubs, and 98 varieties of flowers and plants in the garden — a paradise for the botanical connoisseur. But the home was sold to a developer and threatened with demolition if infill proposals were not promptly approved by City Hall.

Infill homes can be (but are not always) sympathetically designed to blend unobtrusively with existing homes, and in exceptional circumstances City Council can allow increased density on a single family lot where a heritage building is in danger. Indeed, in the absence of legislation to protect heritage listed buildings, allowing infill construction is the city's main tactic to promote preservation of historic homes. In this case local protest persuaded the Planning Department to act and the Haigler House was saved. But the garden was sacrificed and the house moved sideways on its lot to accommodate an undistinguished infill neighbour.

Walking along the foliated avenues of Shaughnessy Heights in Vancouver, you could be forgiven for thinking that you had stumbled into some leafy backwater in suburban England. Everywhere you turn, Tudor gables pop up among the trees. But the turn-of-the-century Tudor Revival style—"stockbroker Tudor" as it was later called in England—wasn't the only style employed by Shaughnessy's builders. Spanish and Dutch Colonial, and Georgian styles were revived during the area's Edwardian heyday. Shaughnessy's architectural character is more diverse than the number of half-timbered Tudor gables suggests.

Shaughnessy Heights was planned in 1907–09 by Danish engineer L. E. Davick and Montreal landscape architect Frederick Todd in the manner of Frederick Law Olmstead, the American landscape architect who designed Central Park, New York and Mount Royal Park, Montreal. The tree-lined streets and capacious villas also owe something to the contemporary influence of the English "garden city movement," an impression enhanced by the area's Tudor Revival/Arts and Crafts architecture.

English influence, via colonial America, is also apparent in a handful of Georgian Revival (or Federal style, as it is called in the US) houses in Shaughnessy. These elegant homes, with their fanlight doors and classical details, are increasingly threatened. This example at 1550 Laurier Avenue, deemed too small by a new owner, was demolished in 1993. Its planned replacement, while conforming to the city's design guidelines for the area, mimics the mock Tudor mansions already common in the neighbourhood.

Sugar magnate B. T. Rogers spent much of his fortune on two lavish Vancouver homes: Gabriola in the West End and then Shannon, built between 1915 and 1925 at 57th Avenue and Granville Street—even grander, but more refined in its historicism. Architects Somervell and Putnam skilfully used their knowledge of classical design to plan this stately home, a villa set on a ten-acre estate to overlook an Italianate garden.

The interior, entered from a vaulted, fan-lit vestibule leading to an arched hallway, has an impressive staircase complete with a Palladian window and neoclassical decor. A baronial fireplace dominates the ballroom while the tiled conservatory suggests sunlit repose. You can still sense the clubby, wood-panelled world of the tycoon and his social circle here, although the mansion has since been converted into suites. Outside, infill dwellings designed by Arthur Erickson and built in 1972, enclose but do not diminish the old house and garden. Significantly, their West Coast modernism complements, rather than imitates, the original Georgian Revival design.

Shannon is given some ostentation by its classical porte-cochere, and a Doric-columned patio which faces the garden. The garden, even in melancholy winter hibernation, is a delight. Its balustraded leafy paths, ornamental ponds, stepped symmetry and regular plantings recall the balance and formal composition that were intended in classical and Renaissance tradition to cultivate the human spirit. Gardens of this type were designed for contemplation and uplifting perambulation: a world where architecture and landscape design were given meaning deeper than the glib pastiche commonplace today.

Gabriola, the West End mansion of sugar baron Benjamin Tingley Rogers, was built at 1531 Davie Street in 1901 to a design by Samuel Maclure. The house is one of the best, and best preserved, of its era in the city. The porte-cochere, richly modelled sandstone friezes carved in the slightly Art Nouveau manner of the famous nineteenth-century American architect Louis Henry Sullivan, a circular corner gazebo, and an asymmetric roof line punctuated by massive stone chimneys, make the house a classic example of late-Victorian picturesque eclecticism,
a term used to describe a building of eccentric personality and enthusiastically distributed, free-ranging styles.

Enough of the original setting, in a park-like garden, remains to give a sense of the carriage-trade world in which Rogers and, indeed, Maclure moved. Maclure was the darling of the well-to-do in Victoria and Vancouver, where he specialized in Tudor Revival mansions designed to flatter and reflect plutocratic privilege and aristocratic yearnings—the sort of milieu where the social season would, in British imperial fashion, revolve around garden parties, soirées with visiting royalty and officers from Royal Navy warships and evenings in the billiard room.

Gabriola is not mock-Tudor, but it is baronial, with an interior in keeping with the Edwardian colonial era of monied leisure and aristocratic pretension. There are huge fireplaces (eighteen at one time), wood-panelled walls and ceilings, ornate plasterwork and a balustered staircase. But the home's *pièce de resistance* is a superb Pre-Raphaelite stained glass window, designed by James Bloomfield, halfway up the grand stairway.

James and his brother Charles Bloomfield were skilled British art glass craftsmen who pioneered stained glass-making in British Columbia. Their business, founded by their father Henry Bloomfield at New Westminster in 1889, manufactured windows for the Parliament Buildings in Victoria and for many private homes, commercial buildings and some churches in the province. Most church glass, requiring a more specialized skill, was imported at the time from Britain, France or eastern Canada.

Stained glass was fashionable around the turn of the century, mainly due to the Arts and Crafts movement and the influence of Victorian Gothic Revival architecture. This style, of which the Parliament Buildings in Ottawa are a classic example, sought inspiration in the cathedrals and craftsmanship of medieval Europe. The Bloomfields' English background and their artistic leanings caused them to maintain, although not extend, this nineteenth-century decorative tradition. They relied on pattern books and clients' taste as much as their own sensibility for their choice of imagery. Much of their work was derivative but occasionally it blossomed, particularly, as can be seen at the Rogers mansion, where the client and architect chose to commission an ambitious figurative piece.

Wood was and still is the most common building material on the West Coast, mainly because of abundant local timber and the ease with which the coastal forests could be logged and used for local buildings. Downtown Vancouver was completely forested until the 1850s when sawmills sprang up to exploit this resource. Sandstone was quarried on Gabriola Island and granite on Haddington Island, but because stone was more expensive than wood and required more skill to carve and fashion as a building material, it was used for public and commercial buildings rather than homes.

Stone houses like this one at 1096 West 10th Avenue (right) are unusual in Vancouver. The house was built in 1911 in inventive Craftsman style with an offset porch and steeply sloping shingled roof. Stone chips inlaid between the half-timbering lend a rural English quality to the home, while its load-bearing granite walls and parapetted window bay seem Scottish and Victorian in inspiration. The projecting window bay below the west gable is an unusual feature more commonly found in Moorish and Mediterranean architecture. The interior incudes a wood-panelled hallway and an amazing kitchen where every surface, including the ceiling, is covered with glazed tiles.

In the 1980s the house was threatened with demolition, but City Council was persuaded to rezone the property from single family residential to office use to accommodate the architectural firm which proposed renovation. In return the architect agreed to the house becoming a city designated heritage building, which, technically, prevents it from unsympathetic alteration or demolition. But despite the benefits, rezoning from residential to any other use frequently raises neighbours' ire (there is often concern about increased traffic), as the city found when it accepted the bequest of Glen Brae, the Shaughnessy mansion, in 1991. Suggestions for Glen Brae included use as city offices and the headquarters for the Heritage Foundation or an arts centre, which would have allowed public access, but Council promptly retreated and the mansion, long used as a sanitorium, is to become a sick children's home.

Some stone houses aren't stone at all. The restored home at 124 West 10th Avenue (below) was built in 1907 with "cast stone" concrete blocks moulded on site to look like the real thing. The adjacent heritage homes on the south side of the block are of traditional wood frame construction. These were rescued from decay in the 1980s by the preservation-minded Davis family, whose energetic community activism ignited a neighbourhood revival subsequently acknowledged and supported by City Hall.

FIRST BAPTIST CHURCH

The First Baptist Church at the corner of Nelson and Burrard streets in Vancouver was designed by the Toronto firm Burke, Horwood & White. Eastern firms were often tempted west by prestige projects where special expertise was thought to be required—although most Edwardian buildings in Vancouver and Victoria were built, quite capably, by local practices.

Edmund Burke's training was with his uncle, Henry Langley, a noted architect in Victorian Toronto who specialized in Gothic Revival churches and homes for the well-to-do. Burke's connections led him to design Simpson's, Toronto's first department store, in 1894, and many Revival style residences for the city's business elite. At the First Baptist Church he used his early experience to compose a stout Gothic Revival building in rusticated granite, anchored to its corner site by a parapetted, buttressed bell tower.

The First Baptists' original church in Vancouver was less imposing. In the 1880s they worshipped in an empty shop in Gastown before moving to a hall at the back of the Blair Saloon at Abbott and Water streets—a not uncommon arrangement in pioneering Vancouver where facilities for prayer and drowning your sorrows could often be found on the same block. A wood frame, steepled church was built in 1889, but the congregation outgrew this and moved to the present stone building, completed in 1911.

In 1932 the First Baptist Church gained a Gothic Revival companion (now St. Andrew's Wesley Church) built on the other side of Nelson Street. The two churches, in an unplanned but pleasing piece of urban design, act as an unexpected, almost processional, gateway to the city's West End.

The Irving House, built in 1862–64 at 302 Royal Avenue, New Westminster, is one of the oldest heritage houses in the province. It was built by Captain William Irving, a Scottish seaman who had settled in Portland, Oregon in 1850 but moved to booming Victoria to cash in on the Cariboo gold rush of 1858. He then moved to the mainland and pioneered sternwheeler steamboat services on the Fraser River, and built the first two vessels of that type to be launched locally. The "King of the River," as he became known, arranged for the Royal Engineers to build his New Westminster home (below) on the slope above the river and the emerging colonial capital (Victoria succeeded New Westminster as the capital in 1871).

A detachment of Royal Engineers had been sent by the Colonial Office in London to select a site for the administration of the newly formed colony of British Columbia.

This resourceful band of soldiers, which included architects, surveyors, engineers and craftsmen, played a leading role in planning, communications, and in maintaining law and order in the developing colony. (Formerly, the Hudson's Bay Company at Fort Victoria had acted as the agent of British influence and authority.) The engineers chose the site for New Westminster, whose name had been chosen by Queen Victoria, and they laid out the town's street grid. Their work is an early example of modern town planning that is often overlooked but still evident—especially directly north of the Irving House in the parks and formal streets of the Queens Park district, a neighbourhood also distinguished by its many fine old homes and potpourri of architectural styles. This 1913 Craftsman style home (below right), to the west of Queens Park at 340 Tenth Street, is a heritage award-winner beautifully

restored by its owners. It is a charming example of the high standard of residential architecture to be found here.

Captain Irving's house was designed in an offshoot of the Gothic Revival style (of late eighteenth- and early nineteenth-century English stately homes) which was popularized from the 1840s to the 1880s in North America by architectural writers and pattern book designs. Examples of Gothic Revival buildings are quite rare on the West Coast. Known as "picturesque" or Carpenter Gothic in North America, the style was used for country homes and cottages. Its rustic, pseudo-medieval qualities were thought to fit well into the landscape.

Most Gothic Revival homes in Canada and the United States were built of wood, and many were decorated with gingerbread carving. The steeply pitched roof, ornamental bargeboards on the gables topped with elaborate finials,

window and doorway mouldings, and bracketed single-storey porch, all seen on the Irving House, are characteristic features. But the Palladian window on the second floor is an unusual classical embellishment. The window once opened onto a rustic balcony, also characteristic but, unfortunately, long ago removed.

The house, now part of the adjacent New Westminster Museum, has been carefully restored. Its interiors are jam-packed with fascinating Victorian bric-a-brac and include some original furnishings, floors laid and caulked as if on the deck of a ship, Italian marble fireplaces, staircase banisters shipped from Scotland, and ornate plasterwork. The house, purchased by the City of New Westminster in 1950, became the borough's first designated heritage home in 1982.

You could walk past St. Paul's Church, in Vancouver's West End, without giving it a second glance. It hardly looks like a great piece of architecture — "pioneer Gothic" would best describe the exterior, completed in 1905. But behind the church's unassuming, rustic shingled walls there is an exquisite columned and panelled wood interior, designed in Gothic Revival style and illuminated by ornamental lamps and some beautiful stained glass windows.

Most of the original glass was made in Vancouver in the style of the local Bloomfield firm, of Gabriola fame. Some came from England, while one window was reputedly manufactured in the New York studio of the celebrated turn-of-the-century American art glass designer Louis Comfort Tiffany. The church's pipe organ, built in 1906 by the Casavant Organ Company, Ste. Hyacinthe, Quebec, is the oldest surviving and continuously played of its type in British Columbia. These relics and the well-preserved original interior give St. Paul's real historic character, comparable to the better-known Christ Church Cathedral, built at the corner of West Georgia and Burrard in 1889–95, also in Gothic Revival style.

The first St. Paul's Mission Church was built in 1889 on the 1200-block Hornby Street on the west edge of Yaletown, an area of warehouses and railway workers' shacks overlooking False Creek. In 1898, when the West End was expanding steadily, the original building was hauled up Davie Street by a team of horses to its present site at the corner of Jervis and Pendrell streets. Remnants of the building were incorporated into the enlarged 1905 design seen today.

St. Paul's Hospital, one of Vancouver's most prominent buildings, was established in 1894 at 1081 Burrard Street by the Sisters of Providence, a Canadian Catholic order founded in 1845. The original Victorian hospital was replaced in 1912 by this block designed by Robert F. Tegen in a decorative Italianate style reminiscent of institutional buildings in nineteenth-century London. There's certainly a Dickensian air to this building which even the charming attempts at decoration—patterned brickwork and terra-cotta details—cannot quite filter away. The gloomy interior, in contrast to that of the new hospital building next door, suggests the old building is well past its prime. Even St. Paul, whose statue guards the hospital from a pedimented niche above the top floor (where five of the sisters live and work), is unlikely to save it from the wrecker's ball. Expansion plans for the hospital do not include renovation.

This is a pity because as well as being a local landmark the 1912 building does have some architectural merit, currently overwhelmed by clumsy 1930s wings and extensions. These should certainly be demolished but the original historic building, with its Romanesque window arches, rich terra-cotta cornice detail, balconies and delightful Tuscan belvedere, could be saved. With a bit of imagination, it could be incorporated into the new plans, either attached to a new building behind or retained, with reinfored backing for the brickwork, as a decorative screen. The result would be something of a folly, but one with more historic substance than the current proposal to destroy the building, saving only the belvedere and planting it in the hospital garden.

Completed in 1912, Chalmers Presbyterian Church in Vancouver was designed in Edwardian classical style, with echoes of the Palladian Revival architecture of stately homes in eighteenth-century England. Samuel Buttrey Birds, the architect of Chalmers, was no Andrea Palladio (the sixteenth-century Italian classicist after whom the style was named). Chalmers is a bit ungainly and would have benefited from a more generous dome and a less flaccid facade on 12th Avenue. The east elevation on Hemlock Street, however, is raised to a noble and palatial scale with a pediment supported on a quartet of Corinthian columns.

Like many churches faced with declining congregations, Chalmers was amalgamated with a neighbour and the building went up for sale in 1991. Gone are the days when ministers like Thomas Chalmers, after whom the church was named, could draw crowds to their services. In nineteenth-century Glasgow, his vigorous sermons were so popular that pews had to be reserved for visitors who travelled to hear him preach.

The building could have been converted into flats, but this would have sacrificed the luminous interior — originally a curving, balconied space with rows of oak pews tumbling down to embrace the organ and altar. Eventually, the building was bought by the Anglican Church and, as Holy Trinity Anglican Church, it is used for its original purpose. Unfortunately the new owners chose not to preserve the interior — a small price to pay, perhaps, for preservation of the overall building. Reconstruction includes a theatre in the undercroft and the restitution of Chalmers' community centre in a new infill building.

The street address of the West Vancouver church St. Francis-in-the-Wood — 4773 Piccadilly South — was named after the famous London thoroughfare by British gentleman, adventurer, artist and scholar Francis Caulfeild. Yet nothing could be further from the real Piccadilly than the village of Caulfeild, established on the edge of the Pacific Ocean in 1899. Francis Caulfeild wrote that it was "a spot they shall not spoil . . . a village of good design according to the contours of nature."

Caulfeild arrived in Vancouver in 1898 after travelling across Canada. He was entranced by the remote, rocky, forested cove he discovered in West Vancouver and set about planning a village, modelled in the English manner with a park, cottages and a church enclosing a village green. The area was almost completely undeveloped at the time, and even today, despite the intrusion of a log cabin monster home (West Vancouver's planners should never have allowed this), you can sense the sylvan beauty that appealed to Caulfeild's cultured, Victorian sensibility.

This delightful nook is given authentic English character by the parish church. The original building (it has since been enlarged) was funded and built in 1926–27 by the villagers of Caulfeild themselves, who had previously worshipped in each other's homes. Henry A. Stone, a local resident and later the founder of the Vancouver Art Gallery, drew up plans for the church, complete with a traditional English lych-gate, and everyone in the small community pitched in to help with the work.

There's a William Morris ring to this story. Caulfeild, with his interest in arts and crafts, was probably influenced by Morris's art and rustic socialism. The name of the church is significant too: St. Francis of Assisi was noted for his "love of nature, reverence for life, and sense of the brotherhood of man," as the church guide puts it. St. Francis is commemorated in a stained glass window, made by Morris and Company, London (founded by William Morris in 1861), that illuminates the soothing interior.

St. Francis of Assisi is also remembered in East Vancouver where the church of St. Francis of Assisi (below) was built on Napier Street, one block east of Victoria Drive. Father Boniface Heidmeier looked to the Franciscan order's spiritual home when he planned this piece of incongruous whimsy set among the frame houses and grander villas of Grandview. Completed in 1938, the church's neo-Romanesque facade and miniature campanile are a vision of the Italy of Renaissance paintings and medieval hill towns.

Wide, flat, bracketed eaves and a three-storey campanile-like tower bring a touch of Tuscany to this unusual villa, thought to have been a show home for the North Vancouver Land and Improvement Company's Ottawa Gardens development. Built in 1907 at 214 West 6th Street, it is one of several Edwardian homes in the neighbourhood—but the only one to be designed in Italianate style.

Italian villa–style homes built during the Edwardian era through to the 1930s were often quite ostentatious and based on formal Renaissance mansions (examples can still be found on Shaughnessy Heights). But this North Vancouver house, although built in 1907, looks more like an Italianate home of the mid-Victorian period. Specifically, it is an example of the "picturesque movement," which originated in Victorian England and also popularized the Gothic Revival style. Here a simplified Renaissance style was blended with the asymmetrical vernacular of Tuscan farmhouses to produce plain but gift-wrapped semi-rural dwellings.

North Vancouver boomed in the Edwardian period. It became known as the "Ambitious City," a result of population growth, feverish land speculation, sawmill and ship-building industries, and port and railway activity. Lower Lonsdale, with its streetcar line and ferry terminal, formed the commercial core of a building boom which never quite made its way up the hill. This area, with its surviving heritage buildings, waterfront activity, new public market and the potential development of the old Wallace Shipyard site, is seeing a revival after years of decline. Still, today's planners, while protecting their heritage, are unlikely to emulate the expansive plans of the Edwardian era. Then, North Vancouver was a community of grand plans—none more so than Grand Boulevard and, to a lesser extent, Ottawa Gardens, both developed by the North Vancouver Land and Improvement Company.

Ottawa Gardens, with its homes on the north and south sides of the street separated by a generous park-like median and anchored at the west end by St. Edmond's Church, is a modest but pleasing example of formal Edwardian town planning. Its scale has been retained in the variety of residential architecture here—from Edwardian to the present day—and the way in which the different styles conform to the character of the district.

Grand Boulevard, developed around the same time, also displays a variety of styles—from Tudor Revival to 1960s ranch-style bungalows—but was planned on a much more ambitious scale. Presenting a broad vista sloping from the mountains toward the sea, nearly a mile long and 350 feet wide, Grand Boulevard lives up to its name. It was billed as the "Champs Elysées" of the West Coast. But the depression of 1912 prevented architectural development on the anticipated scale. Only handful of Edwardian mansions which dot its periphery, and the imperial scale of the street plan—now incongruously suburban—give a sense of what might have been.

This east Vancouver building looks as if it were built for the pleasure of some Spanish nobleman or a Hollywood film star, rather than as the Girls' Industrial School, a reform school for wayward girls, which used the building until 1959. The building at 800 Cassiar Street was designed in a style which suggests anything but institutional use.

Constructed in 1912, it is one of the earliest and best examples of Spanish Mission style architecture in the province. Currently the unexpectedly romantic location of provincial social services offices, the building still stands much as built (minus a cupola once centred on the roof) in its original setting with a semi-circular driveway and manicured front lawn.

Spanish Mission and Colonial Revival buildings are quite rare in British Columbia. Most can be found in Vancouver where the market was large enough to accommodate fashionable whimsy from California. Both styles originated there, inspired by the eighteenth-century Spanish presence in the American southwest.

Graceful, shaped gables on the two projecting wings (repeated in miniature in the half-dormers) and the arcaded loggia are identifying features of the Mission Revival style here — a style of the Edwardian era which can be distinguished from the later Spanish Colonial Revival style of the 1920s, with which it is often confused — by the relative absence of exterior decoration. Mission facades were plain and usually stuccoed. Both styles used tiles for floors, wall decoration and roofs. In Vancouver the two related styles were freely interpreted, often in an engaging blend of Mexico and the Mediterranean.

This exuberant Spanish Colonial Revival block, at 1101 Nicola Street in Vancouver's West End, evokes the urban California of Raymond Chandler blended with the European Belle Epoque. When built in 1928 by the Dominion Construction Company, the reinforced concrete building boasted "Vancouver's finest furnished and unfurnished apartments." Indeed, the structure has the scale and presence of a *fin-de-siècle* European apartment block of a type still found from Barcelona to Budapest. Inside, the flats' classical mouldings, Adam fireplaces, high ceilings and parquet floors enhance the effect.

The Queen Charlotte deserves the city heritage award it won in 1993. Virtually every detail of this grand edifice has been preserved in original condition, or has been restored in keeping with its 1920s design. Overhanging tiled eaves, shaped gables and a two-storey main entrance (decorated with a Moorish tiled dado and Castilian wrought-iron light fittings) emphasize the Queen Charlotte's Spanish Colonial character, although the name recalls British royalty. Roughly stuccoed walls and original sash windows add to the building's authenticity.

Beyond the entrance, with its bevelled glass and gilt swash lettering, the lobby decor mixes Spanish Colonial and Art Deco motifs. The former foyer reception lounge (now enclosed in one of the ground floor suites), with its Persian carpets and Moorish arched wall niches, looked like an emir's chamber in some alcazar in southern Spain. But the building's most unusual period feature is its original elevator — the sort which, in old department stores and office buildings, always had an elderly operator to press the buttons and open and close the concertina gates.

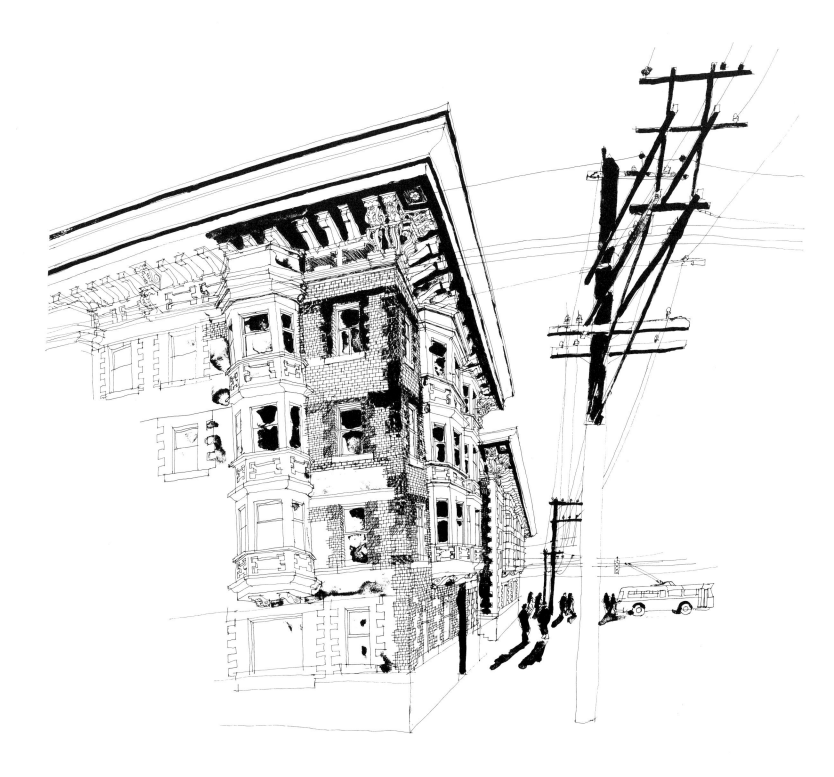

Architects Parr and Fee were among the most prolific designers in Edwardian Vancouver. They built mansions in Shaughnessy like Glen Brae and the occasional bombastic commercial block. The remarkable terra-cotta-clad Vancouver Block (on Granville Street just south of Georgia) is the most spectacular example of the latter. But their bread and butter work was warehouses, hotels and apartment blocks, many of which still stand in the city. These buildings are characterized by classical proportions, regular fenestration and brick facades enlivened by Parr and Fee's favourite topping. They loved cornices.

The cornice detail on Manhattan Apartments, on the northeast corner of Robson Street at Thurlow, is their tour de force. Here, bold, double-barrelled brackets lushly carved with acanthus leaves (a classical Greek motif) support an emphatic, projecting cornice. Three storeys of stained glass rise above the main door set in a pilastered, recessed entrance bay. Oriel windows rippling along the elevations bring further variety and visual interest to the inventive design.

Manhattan Apartments were built in 1908. The building was one of the earliest apartment buildings in the West End and one of the first to increase available natural light by setting the entrance back in a courtyard, an idea which was quickly imitated on similar buildings in the city, mostly in the West End. Renovations carried out after residents saved the building from the wrecker's ball in the 1970s have cleverly highlighted this feature. The narrow courtyard has been opened out to form a terrace and columned passage — a pleasant, human-scale urban space reminiscent of the intimate, nineteenth-century arcades one

finds in Paris and other European cities. Oddly, the telegraph poles, which survive on Thurlow Street, visually return the Manhattan to its 1908 North American urban context. Their frontier vitality serves as a symbol of the chaotic, boomtown period when the Manhattan was built.

Also in the West End, architect Thomas A. Fee's house, built in 1903, still stands at the corner of Broughton and Pendrell streets. The house was a practice run for his later, more elaborate West End home on Gilford Street, built in 1907, now long gone. Fee's house, dilapidated for some time, has recently been moved flush to the corner of its site to await renovation and to allow an infill development by the current owner. With its typical Parr and Fee turretted corner, it an important example of period architecture in the West End and of the architects' residential work — which reached a romantic apogee at Glen Brae.

There's a dramatic juxtaposition of old and new here that was not intended when BC Hydro began to acquire and demolish old properties on the downtown Vancouver block bounded by Dunsmuir, Homer, Hamilton and Pender streets. Hydro planned to clear the block from Dunsmuir Street to the lane half a block north, to make way for their new office tower. But they didn't count on having to deal with the owner of the Del Mar Hotel.

Most of us, if offered the equivalent of several suitcases of cash for an old hotel, might be tempted to speak to a Swiss bank or plan winters in Mexico. But the owner of the Del Mar was proud of his Edwardian hotel, the last original building on the BC Hydro site. He rebuffed all offers to buy, forcing Hydro to alter the position — but, unfortunately, not the appearance — of their new tower, a dated example of postmodernism.

The Del Mar proprietor's social conscience was clearly more developed than his business sense. He had been providing clean, affordable accommodation for Downtown Eastside residents for twenty years and decided that he wished to continue doing so. The Contemporary Art Gallery, located on the Del Mar's ground floor, erected a typographic artwork above their entrance to commemorate this small victory of human over corporate values. It reads *Unlimited Growth Increases the Divide* — a potent graffito which is to remain on the Del Mar as long as the building stands.

The Downtown Eastside, which centres along Hastings Street from the Victory Square district to beyond Main Street, is the long-neglected centre of old downtown Vancouver. Here you will find some of Vancouver's finest heritage buildings, and Edwardian streetscapes unaltered for years. The area is also home to low-income Vancouverites, many of them elderly, who can't afford anything better or who choose to stay because it's the neighbourhood they know.

Development like the BC Hydro Building, which displaces people and threatens heritage architecture, is neither welcome nor appropriate anywhere near historic Victory Square. A mixed-use, mid-rise, high-density development maintaining the existing street elevations but dissolving inside into courtyards, galleries and arcades — in the manner of the Sinclair Centre, for example — would have been a more stimulating response to the site than the cliché that was built.

Almost as distressing as the mass of the BC Hydro tower is its style. What an astonishing lapse in the standard of corporate patronage of the arts this building represents. In 1957, BC Hydro were proud owners of a futuristic tower they had commissioned at the corner of Nelson and Burrard streets — still one of the finest modern buildings in the city. In 1993 the best they can boast is a bloated piece of postmodernism, supposedly representing the mountains and waterfalls from which the utility draws its power but failing to capture either the fluidity of the resource or the high technology Hydro employs to deliver its service.

UNLIMITED GROWTH INCREASES THE DIVIDE

JUSTICE
THIS PROPERTY
IS NOT FOR
SALE AND IT
HAS NOT BEEN
SOLD. THANK YOU
THE OWNER

DEL-MAR HOTEL

VACANCY

CONTEMPORARY ART GALLERY
555

555
DEL MAR
HOTEL

TALL CRANE

PCN
SITE OFFICE
SECOND FLOOR

THIS IS A
HARD HAT
AREA

CATHEDRAL PLACE
Georgia Medical–Dental Building
Marine Building
Northern Life Building, Seattle

Cathedral Place, the much-heralded new addition to Vancouver's skyline at 925 West Georgia Street, is a modern office tower disguised to look like a cross between the 1929 Georgia Medical–Dental Building it replaced in 1990 (amid much controversy) and the Hotel Vancouver, from the same era, across the street. The Marine Building, which was refurbished by Cathedral Place's architect, Paul Merrick, also figures in the new building's multi-facetted postmodernism, rooting Cathedral Place firmly in the familiar details of neighbouring heritage buildings. This fact helped ease the project through the planning stage despite vocal opposition from those who preferred its Art Deco predecessor.

It is acceptable architectural practice today to recall the past after obliterating its monuments. Indeed, planning departments encourage developers and architects to do this, and all concerned advance a persuasive argument that recollecting the old in the new helps maintain continuity in the urban environment. Cathedral Place seems to be gaining acceptance and popularity for this reason. But in purely architectural and intellectual terms, does it deserve to? There's an element of sophistry in the idea that you show respect for the past by replicating it in new construction. The only way to respect the past is to keep it.

Imitating the past does nothing to promote good contemporary architecture. Cathedral Place, beneath its faux historical decor, is an elegant modern design. While it may have been desirable to commemorate the passing of the Georgia Medical–Dental Building, it was not necessary, except to placate the heritage lobby and indulge the architect's whimsy, to stick bits of it onto the new tower. The imitation terra-cotta lions, nurses, griffins and gar-

goyles, and the fussy balcony railings, detract from the building's robust composition.

Some aspects of the old building—its setback massing, firm relationship to the street and overall scale—were worth reinterpreting and improving upon. Indeed, Cathedral Place's redeeming qualities owe much to the old building and to architect Merrick and developer Ron Shon's willingness to let it define the new. The granite-faced ground floor, the modelling of the window bays, the glazed corners rising and multiplying as setbacks and receding into a stone crown topped by a chateauesque pinnacle, help Cathedral Place overcome its ill-chosen surface decoration. The aspects of the past which work well here do so because they have become part of the local architectural vocabulary and have been applied, broadly, in context.

The chateauesque roof complements the Hotel Vancouver's copper peak, and its shape is something of a Canadian icon—some might say cliché—much abused on lesser buildings. At Cathedral Place it is the dominant feature, a Canadian tradition which recalls the monumental Canadian Pacific Railway hotels of the late nineteenth century. In its shape, setbacks, and lobby and entrances flush to the street, Cathedral Place also reworks the conventions of classic North American skyscrapers of the 1920s and 1930s. It is reassuringly traditional, even old-fashioned, in this respect, although the stylized gargoyles and griffins, inspired respectively by ornaments on the Hotel Vancouver and the Chrysler Building in New York, introduce a coy historicism which would have been better left on the drawing board.

The Georgia Medical–Dental Building fell short of true skyscraper status, but Cathedral Place, with its roof peak-ing above twenty-four storeys, sucessfully achieves it. Where the old building presented a respectable face only to Georgia and Hornby streets (its north and west facades were left unfinished, anticipating neighbours never built), the new tower restores these incomplete facings and shows what the Georgia Medical's architects, McCarter & Nairne, might have done had they been asked to fully dress the original building.

The fact that the Georgia Medical–Dental Building was not fully completed effectively sealed its fate. Comparisons were drawn with the same architects' Marine Building, a few blocks away, which is a more lavish and confident example of the Art Deco style. But the Georgia Medical–Dental Building was important. It had a melange of Art Deco detail — geometric terra-cotta panels and three sphinx-like nurses (higher up on the corners than their replicas have now been placed) — not noticed by people who had bad memories of dental treatment there. Above the vaulted doorway, quasi-religious panels illustrated the medical profession at work. The lobby was decorated in the Mayan/ Hollywood style fashionable at the time.

No amount of recasting and rearranging copied components of the old can replace the singular contribution to the streetscape and city life which old buildings make. The Georgia Medical–Dental Building was an authentic example of Art Deco. Its brick facade, concealing a reinforced concrete frame, and terra-cotta details had weathered to a comfortable patina. Where the building failed the test of time was that its interior spaces could not keep up to central business district standards of efficiency or financial return. Yet the building could have been upgraded with a modern infill behind. All that now survives from the origi-

nal building are assorted pieces of terra-cotta in the Vancouver Museum and in private collections. Ironically, salvaged terra-cotta from the building was sold in 1992 to raise funds for the city's heritage foundation.

Panels from the building's entrance arch were also saved. They have been preserved and reinstated, not inappropriately, inside the Canadian Craft Museum, a scaled down echo of Cathedral Place across a garden courtyard from the tower. Thoughtful planning of this public space, with its arbored walkways and sense of privacy — a false wall on Hornby Street, shored up by six sturdy buttresses, provides some seclusion to the garden — has done much to humanize the development, permitting pedestrian access and enriching the urban texture. Wood, though, rather than steel — this is the West Coast, after all — would have been a more harmonious material to have framed the pathways.

Facing the courtyard, the south wall of the craft museum is embellished with an Art Deco screen cast from the Georgia Medical–Dental Building's top-storey terra-cotta corona, but, as with every other replicated relic of the old building, the original spatial, architectural and historic context has evaporated. The craft museum also boasts a chateauesque roof, reinforcing the impression that the Cathedral Place project is not architecture at all but a theme park.

In the lobby of the tower, the striking, luminous two-storey hall is designed in what can best be described as neo-medieval/expressionist style. This Gothic foyer, complete with false columns and cathedral-like windows, seems to have been inspired by Christ Church Cathedral, the tiny Gothic Revival church next door begun in 1889, from

GOING OUT OF BUSINESS GOING OUT OF BUSINESS

da Carlo
RISTORANTE ITALIANO

ORIENTAL RUGS

ORIENTAL RUG BAZAAR

P
A
R
K

which Cathedral Place draws its name. But there is nothing of the spiritual or contemplative aura, nor the craftsmanship, of English parish churches or European Gothic cathedrals to which Cathedral Place so cavalierly refers. Cathedral Place's medievalism, like that of the Hotel Vancouver, is a highly marketable sham.

"Timelessness" is the quality with which the developer asked his architect to imbue Cathedral Place. The word suggests the sublime and eternal, but only buildings of exquisite formality or individual creative expression resonate in this way—the austere MacMillan Bloedel Building a block west on Georgia Street, designed by Arthur Erickson in the late 1960s, is a good local example. Cathedral Place's postmodernism, layered with whimsical historic reference, is very much a building of its own time. Like the Hotel Vancouver, it seems destined to become a case study for architecture historians and students. It may even become a heritage building. For the public, who will wonder what those nurses are doing up there, it will always be something of a curiosity.

Cathedral Place, while trapped by its predecessor in a bizarre stylistic limbo, does represent a significant act of architectural patronage. Both developer and architect wished to create a landmark building which would reflect artistic as well as commercial interests—a cultural commitment which can be traced back to the Renaissance. The Georgia Medical–Dental Building's architects, McCarter & Nairne, worked within this tradition—where buildings had more meaning than just dollars and cents—but at a time when the decorative arts still had some social and cultural relevance to architectural design. In Vancouver this traditional decorative symbolism is most fully and confidently realized in McCarter & Nairne's finest creation, one of Canada's best Art Deco buildings: the Marine Building, completed in 1930 at 355 Burrard Street.

J. Y. McCarter worked as a logger and was a boxer, an engineer and an officer in the Royal Navy during World War One before he turned to architecture. George Nairne was an itinerant theatre designer who worked in Glasgow, New York and Seattle before entering a partnership with McCarter in Vancouver. McCarter's maritime experience and Nairne's sense of theatre were given full rein at the Marine Building—with spectacular results.

When the Marine Building was opened in 1930 the architects explained: "Its architectural conception . . . suggests some great marine rock rising from the sea, clinging with sea flora and fauna, in sea green flashed with gold." McCarter & Nairne went overboard designing decoration to represent Vancouver's emerging status as a major port (the building's original tenants included the city's main shipping and marine insurance companies, and lumber, grain and import–export merchants). Terra-cotta friezes of Neptune and his creatures ripple across the facade like high-water marks. Panels on the lower walls depict the transportation of the day: zeppelins, other aircraft, steamships and trains. The entrance arch, with navigator George Vancouver's ship sailing out of an Art Deco sunrise, is embellished with bas-relief panels illustrating the argosies of West Coast maritime history, from Spanish galleons to the Canadian Pacific Railway's illustrious Empress liners which once sailed from Vancouver's downtown piers to the Orient.

The foyer is a tour de force of 1930s decor—a vaulted two-storey hall ablaze with light fittings like ships' prows breaking through the walls. The floor is decorated with a marble astrological chart, originally linoleum, suggestive of voyages on predestined courses. The linoleum was removed to the Vancouver Museum during a 1989 remodelling, a move criticized by heritage purists who felt the replacement of a perfectly serviceable fitting was a desecration of the building's heritage character. The elevators, their doors awash with undersea flora, are beautifully detailed with Art Deco marquetry. In the 1930s the lifts were operated by young women in sailor suits. But the Marine Building is not theme park architecture. The decoration is applied with consistency and in the mainstream style of the period. It represents a high point of architectural applied art and craftsmanship.

Art Deco's ziggurats, zigzags, cascading waterfalls, sunbursts and futuristic geometry, fashioned in terra-cotta, marble and stone, could not be re-created today except at prohibitive expense. Named after an exhibition of decorative and industrial art held in Paris in 1925, Art Deco blended classical Greek and Egyptian forms with jazz age imagery, the angular and streamlined shapes of cubist painting, modern architecture, industry and transport. In North America the style was enriched by the influence of Mayan art (rediscovered at the time, like Tutankhamen's Egypt) and Hollywood set design: the Marine Building's penthouse, sitting atop the building's steel frame, is shaped in Mayan temple style.

Buildings sprang up all across the continent clad in expressive futuristic or elaborately arcane ornament. Seattle's rival to the Marine Building, the Northern Life Tower at 1218 Third Avenue, makes an interesting comparison between the responses of two different architects to similar sites in similar Pacific coast cities. Both buildings were built at the same time in the same Art Deco skyscraper style, surging skywards in shafts and setbacks. But where the Marine Building was conceived as "some great rock rising from the sea," the Northern Life Building's architects, Albertson, Wilson and Richardson, described a darker vision. Like nearby Mount Rainier, Albertson said at the time, the Northern Life Building was to rise "out of the ground . . . white at the top with perpetual snow" cascading downward "into the deep evergreen of the forests below."

The building's brickwork, like that on the Marine Building, is beautifully crafted and was graded light to dark to heighten the allusion, moody and Nordic in its effect, to an impenetrable forested interior. Three conifer-shaped iron finials on top of the tower further emphasize the point. At street level, a richly decorated, cavernous lobby tunnels its way into the heart of the building. Here, a gilt bas-relief of the Pacific Ocean, alive with neocolonial symbols — the aircraft and steamships of the 1920s American economic empire — celebrates seaborne trade and transport.

The dark mood of the Seattle building's exterior was not intended at the time. The Northern Life Tower was originally illuminated by more than two hundred lights in its recessed spaces, "simulating the aurora borealis." Perhaps it is today's looming environmental catastrophes that overlay its forested symbolism with a powerful, gloomy resonance. The Marine Building, by comparison, still seems fresh and unpolluted and limitless, as we fondly imagine the oceans to be.

What both buildings share is the hopeful spirit of their era, expressed with a stylistic swagger which puts postmodern imitators like Cathedral Place firmly in their place.

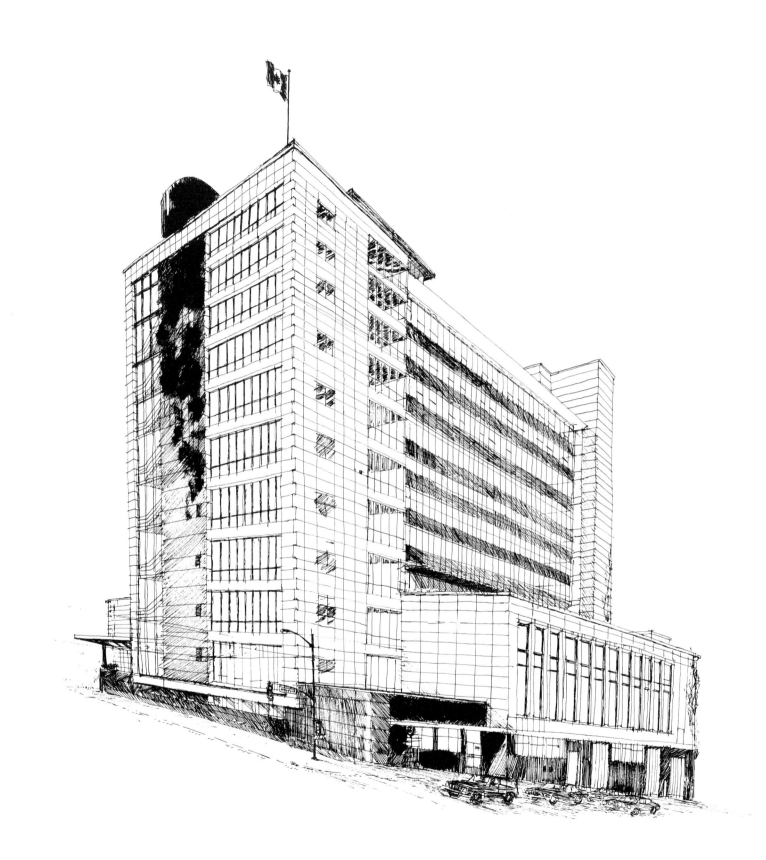

Art Deco, with its popular, futuristic decor, was the acceptable face of modernism between the wars. Buildings from this and earlier periods are generally perceived as having some heritage value, and efforts are generally made to preserve them. It is more difficult to make a case for a postwar buildings, particularly because modern architecture has fallen so low in public (and Royal) esteem. But some modern buildings deserve reappraisal. As examples of a particular period and form of architectural expression the best examples will, if they survive, become the heritage buildings of the future.

Vancouver has a small — and diminishing — collection of postwar buildings designed in the International style — the classic, unadorned functional style which, in the best examples, can be admired for refinement, precision, elegance and clarity. These include the old BC Hydro Building (Nelson and Burrard), the public library (Robson and Burrard), the Guinness Tower (West Hastings), the Canadian Imperial Bank of Commerce (Granville and Dunsmuir) and, until recently, the Customs Building (Hastings and Burrard). Buildings of this type need to be judged not by current postmodern taste but in the broader context of architectural and social history.

The origins of the International style can be traced back to Europe in the early 1900s when radical architects questioned the need for modern industrial society to make its buildings look like Roman palazzos or Greek temples. They rebelled against the suffocating historicism of the late-Victorian era, and their work was controversial from the start: Austria's Emperor Franz Josef was so appalled when modernist architect Adolf Loos built a stark new building outside his baroque Viennese palace in 1911, that he had the curtains permanently drawn. But the movement away from decoration gathered strength after World War One, influenced by the Bauhaus school of design in Germany and the revolutionary Russian avant-garde of the 1920s. The so-called Modern movement began to influence design in North America in the 1930s, drifting to Vancouver after the war.

These modern buildings were built at a time when there was still faith in the future and in technology's capacity to solve, rather than contribute to, man's problems. Their functional forms, while unadorned, were often complemented by works of art, maintaining the symbolic tradition that had previously been served by ornamental stone and terra-cotta. A striking example is the CIBC banking hall mural, in Venetian mosaic by local artist B. C. Binning, with its emphatic celebration of capital and labour, and arts and crafts in British Columbia.

Abstract mosaics, also by Binning, can be seen on the BC Hydro Building, itself the subject of a heritage debate. Disowned by Hydro, the building is to be converted to residential use, which will affect its appearance. The Hydro Building received heritage designation, but its curtain wall is to be replaced. Unfortunately, debate failed to save the Customs Building, an early flagship of modernism built in 1948 whose energetic geometry contrasted with the Marine Building across the street. The Customs Building was demolished in 1993, ironically just after the City of Vancouver's Planning Department had compiled an inventory of post-1940 buildings to be considered for future preservation.

The Standard Building, built in 1914 at 510 West Hastings Street, is a prominent relic of Edwardian Vancouver. It's not a particularly elegant building, impressive more for its size—fifteen storeys of steel frame clad in brick and ornamental terra-cotta—than architectural sophistication. The neoclassical facade rises fourteen storeys to a flourish of Gothic terra-cotta on the top floor, a fashionable addition influenced by New York's neo-Gothic Woolworth Building of the same period. The result, though, is a forced marriage of the two styles. The top floor lacks the panache which would have given the building true eccentricity, although the original plans did call for a more elaborate treatment here.

Still, the building is an interesting period piece, made more attractive by recent rehabilitation on the ground floor. The lobby, a florid example of Edwardiana, has been restored to its past exuberance. In this wildly indulgent foyer, you can sense the vigour and confidence of the city at the time. Something of this confidence, and a certain nobility, can also be seen in the lobby display of old photographs recording the building's construction. The rebuilt main floor has extended the lobby in a pleasing spatial sequence to an adjacent espresso bar. The sociable conversion of the former banking hall—fine ceiling plasterwork here—recognizes the traditional blend of tenants (retail space is also included) that gave variety and dense, gregarious character to Edwardian office blocks and city life generally.

A more radical rehabilitation saved the Randall Building (right), at 555 West Georgia, from demolition. Because the Standard Building was built to a higher density than would be permitted today, there was an incentive to main-

tain it for its rental value. The Randall Building, being smaller, was more vulnerable to change. Rezoning to allow for a "heritage density bonus," whereby the developer gains higher density, building height, floor space and so on, in return for retaining an old building, can save heritage buildings—or at least their facades.

Tony Cavelti, a local jeweller, saw the 1928 building's period charm (its lower floors are clad in Art Deco/heraldic Gothic style terra-cotta) and negotiated a heritage density bonus for an additional top floor on the rebuilt interior. Exterior restoration was then affordable, and the owner accepted heritage designation for the building. This latter point is significant, because unless property owners and developers can be given an incentive to encourage designation, there is little (in the absence of outright grants or legislation) that the city can do to ensure preservation.

STANDARD BUILDING

VANCOUVER PENS

SINCLAIR CENTRE
General Post Office

The Sinclair Centre was the most ambitious heritage restoration and renewal scheme in Vancouver in the 1980s, and it remains the benchmark by which such work should be judged. Care was taken to preserve the Edwardian streetscapes—there are no inappropriate modern excrescences poking through the roofs of the old buildings and no contemporary "heritage" details to compromise their character.

This exemplary project, by the federal agency Public Works Canada and architects Henriquez & Partners, involved the "adaptive reuse" of a complete city block, bounded by Granville, West Hastings, Cordova and Howe streets, and the four heritage buildings which define its corners and streetscapes. The four buildings' facades were retained, along with some sense of their internal structure, but were otherwise rebuilt inside with modern offices and a bijou shopping arcade intriguingly layered behind the restored facades. The architects wisely resisted the temptation to mimic the heritage buildings' styles and opted for a clear demarcation between the old and the new. While the steel and glass of the arcade and galleria are reminiscent of nineteenth-century precedents—and an appropriate way to internally link the old buildings—the unadorned, robust construction of the arcade and galleria (steel and exposed concrete pillars) counterpoints the more delicate period notes struck by the heritage buildings' decorative details, which have been judiciously recycled throughout.

The four heritage buildings are notable for their quality and variety of styles: the former General Post Office, built at Hastings and Granville in 1905–10 by the Department of Public Works in Beaux Arts style, is stout with neoclassical stonework; the Federal Building, built as the post office

extension in 1935–39 by architects McCarter & Nairne, is a dignified classical design embellished with Art Deco relief work; the Customs Examining Warehouse, although built in 1911–13, has the dour industrial character of Victorian England; the Winch Building which, with the General Post Office, forms the central business district's best preserved Edwardian streetscape, is a grand neo-Renaissance palazzo built by a local business baron in 1908–09.

The most impressive and ebullient of the Sinclair Centre's heritage buildings is the General Post Office (left). Its superb Beaux Arts design is Vancouver's most imposing and convincing example of the style, named after the Ecole des Beaux Arts in Paris, the premier school of architecture in Europe in the late nineteenth century, which budding architects in Europe and North America aspired to attend. The well-handled corner sequence, which anchors the composition's rusticated arcades and colonnades to the sloping site, rises through paired classical columns (a hallmark of the Beaux Arts style) and curved pediments to a domed clock tower, topped by a delightful cupola with a sailing ship on the weathervane. The Parisian mansard roof adds further Gallic flair to the design. But the old post office also has a rather pompous but likable British colonial air—the Beaux Arts style's overblown, decorative classicism was much favoured by governments and public institutions of the period.

In architect Francis Rattenbury's vision of Victoria as an "imperial garden of Eden" dotted with picturesque and monumental buildings, the city was always meant to be seen from the sea. Around the turn of the century most visitors arrived in Victoria by steamer; this is still the best way to first glimpse British Columbia's provincial capital. Few ships captured the romance of this approach to the inner harbour better than the *Princess Marguerite*.

Like most ships in Canadian Pacific's magnificent fleet of coastal steamers and ocean-going Empress liners, she was built in Scotland, at the Fairfield shipyard in Glasgow. While technically up-to-date when launched in 1948, her elegant lines showed the classic prewar styling of her similarly named predecessor, which had been torpedoed in the Mediterranean in 1942. Although modified over the decades, some of her dated, Clydebuilt splendour survived into recent years. The dining room with its etched mirrors, inlaid wood panelling, and Art Deco lighting was straight out of the 1930s. White tablecloths, clinking china and smartly uniformed stewards suggested a bygone era of languid voyages and shipboard romance. Down below, the engine room and the steam turbine engines were in immaculate, almost original condition—the *Princess Marguerite* had steamed only a fraction of her expected mileage.

In the 1950s she sailed on the Vancouver–Victoria route and, briefly, was used as an Alaska cruise ship. From the 1960s up to her early retirement in 1989, when she was withdrawn from service and, subsequently, towed to an uncertain fate in the far east, she steamed between Seattle and Victoria (from 1975–88 as the BC government's flagship), giving many visitors a memorable first impression of Victoria's architecture and setting. While appealing to passengers, the *Princess Marguerite*'s unique period charm, local historic significance, and potential as a museum ship were, sadly, not seen by the provincial and municipal governments of the day. They failed to provide the leadership to retain the vessel after it had been sold to a private shipping company in 1988 and subsequently withdrawn from service.

Whatever ship you're on, though, rounding Laurel Point into the tidal arena of James Bay is a thrilling experience—"halfway between Balmoral and Heaven," as Princess Louise once declared. Despite some impertinent additions to the skyline—and fatuous postmodern development on the port side as you sail in—the inner harbour, dead ahead and to starboard, still presents a panoply of Victoriana. It is a tableau dominated, as Rattenbury intended, by his provincial Parliament Buildings, completed in 1897 and designed in enjoyable late-Victorian eclectic style, and the majestic, chateauesque Empress Hotel of 1908. Facing the hotel, also erected in true imperial fashion, there is a statue of Captain James Cook, the British navigator who explored the West Coast in 1778.

The city lobbied the CPR to build the hotel, which for all its grandeur became something of a consolation prize after Vancouver was named the terminus of Canadian Pacific's transcontinental railway in 1886, although a more northerly route, crossing to the island to terminate at Victoria, had been proposed. But what a prize! The railway spared no expense in fitting out the hotel, which quickly became popular with local high society, well-to-do European tourists, and naval and colonial officers (both Victoria and Vancouver were on the so-called "all red route" from Britain, across Canada, to colonies in Asia). A 1930 CPR

brochure, now in the hotel's archive display, compares the "stately hostelry to a castle of antiquity . . . nestling on the harbour edge." But by the late 1980s the Empress had become something of an aging diva, singing out her declining years on the strength of her reputation.

Behind the facade's ivy curtain, the foyer, with its traditional afternoon tea service, had become a chaotic scene — luggage all over the place, guests trying to check in, bewildered tourists agog at the glorious but faded decor, harassed bellboys and waitresses, and indignant, tweedy locals tut-tutting from behind the potted palms. As for the fabled dining room, once the haunt of commodores, brigadiers and other echelons of Britain's imperial aristocracy, well, the kippers had never swum in Loch Fyne.

In 1988 Canadian Pacific Hotels closed the hotel for a six-month, $45-million restoration and upgrading, part of an ambitious scheme to renovate the company's unique collection of heritage hotels across the country. A new general manager was appointed to reverse years of underinvestment, and to improve staff morale, standards of service and the physical character and layout of the building. The most radical alteration was the addition of a new reception hall, built in front of the 1929 Humboldt Wing, which allowed restoration of the original lobby's gilded Edwardian decor, the setting for the 100,000 afternoon teas served to visitors every year.

The addition of the new lobby, and an elevator tower behind (which has added a further chateauesque feature to the building's extraordinary roof line), did not pass unnoticed in a town that considers the Empress its own and where any tinkering with the regal edifice is seen as an act of lese majesty. But the new structures seem in keeping with the character of the hotel, itself a series of additions to Rattenbury's original central facade. CP searched as far away as Spain in an attempt to match the original Welsh slate for the elevator tower, an example of the attention to detail and consideration for the original design that was the guiding principle of the renovations. The most visible change, though, was the removal of much of the ivy that had colonized the facade over the years. This did give the building a colourful, topiary quality, as if it had been designed by an ambitious gardener rather than an architect. The ivy, which had begun to damage the brickwork, will grow back. Meanwhile, architectural details not seen for years have been revealed.

Rattenbury had arrived in British Columbia a relatively inexperienced Englishman, and had blossomed into precocious maturity with his confident, imperial design for the Parliament Buildings in 1897. There he displayed his penchant for fashionably Victorian "picturesque eclecticism," mixing historic styles — Classical and Romanesque, in this case — with the confident abandon of the times. At the Empress, he slightly anglified the Franco-Scottish chateau style which the Montreal-based Canadian Pacific Railway had made its own. Rattenbury had been given a tour of Le Château Frontenac, opened in Quebec City in 1893, and during his tour, Canadian Pacific officials politely instructed him to refer to this structure when composing the Empress. Rattenbury acted in the spirit, rather than to the letter, of the instruction by ignoring the Frontenac's asymmetrical massing in favour of a formal facade more in keeping with his vision of Victoria's harbour. It is the additions by other architects that have given the Empress the rambling roofscape that is associated with the CPR style.

Inside, his grand public spaces, decorated in an array of styles, are a catalogue of contemporary taste. The colonial Bengal Room, where you can still sample the curry tiffin, comes complete with a deceased tiger mounted on the wall. Hunting prints, Scottish Highland landscapes, a stag's head and heraldic stained glass decorate the heavily panelled lounge and dining room, where a baronial fireplace still dominates the linen and silver settings. The old lobby where tea is served is palatial in its extravagance. Indeed, the whole building is a potpourri of antique features—Adamesque scrollwork, classical columns, oak panelling, brass Art Nouveau fireplace details, and, finest of all, a Tiffany-style stained glass dome which illuminates the Palm Court. This piece, once damaged by an unusually heavy snowfall and boarded up long ago, was rediscovered and repaired during the hotel's renovation, much to the amazement and delight of hotel staff, visitors and guests.

Rattenbury's personal and professional life took irreversible tumbles in the 1920s and he retired to England, where he was bumped off by his chauffeur and wife's paramour in an Agatha Christie setting in Bournemouth. But in the early years of the century, he was the toast of Victoria society. His clients included the CPR, the Bank of Montreal and the Grand Trunk Pacific Railway (now Canadian National), for whom he planned a gigantic chateau-style hotel in Prince Rupert. (World War One consigned this project to the provincial archives, where the drawings can still be seen.) In an unusual neoclassical mood he designed the Edwardian courthouse in Vancouver (now the Vancouver Art Gallery) and the CPR Steamship Terminal in Victoria, his swan song, built in 1924.

One of his most attractive works is the old Bank of Montreal (left) at Government and View streets in Victoria, a richly textured 1897 building. Rattenbury's smaller buildings look like picturesque follies, designed not to be banks or courthouses but imaginary castles. His Nanaimo courthouse was styled as a miniature French chateau. The one in Nelson is more Scottish baronial. For the Bank of Montreal he concocted a blend of Renaissance and Romanesque, sketching in castellated parapets, rusticated stonework, foliated friezes, gargoyles, and a chateau-style roof in the eclectic manner fashionable in the late Victorian era. There's an ineffable quality to this design that tells you the architect enjoyed himself here, so much so that he reworked the style and some features of the bank when he drew up plans for the Empress Hotel.

Victoria has one of the finest groupings of turn-of-the-century architecture in Canada, far greater in range and quality than, for example, arch rival Vancouver. Virtually all the city centre streets are lined with facades of architectural interest and charm. Victoria's late nineteenth-century brick and stone shops, warehouses and banks were generally built to a uniform scale. None completely overpowers its neighbour, yet each building expresses the taste and idiosyncrasies of its architect or owner. Chinese recessed balconies, classical columns, baronial turrets and heavenly spires jostle in lively and pleasingly incongruous ensemble. Government Street has a particularly rich display of styles—everything from E. A. Morris Tobacconist's Arts and Crafts style shopfront, with delightful period typography and a rare, original interior, to Munro's Books, an excellent example of sympathetic reuse of a redundant heritage building (formerly the Royal Bank of Canada, built in 1909), and the late Victorian heritage buildings of nearby Market Square (right). Bastion Square, with its trees, wynds and vista of the sea framed by the 1889 courthouse (now the Maritime Museum; inside is a splendid Victorian open cage elevator, the oldest still working in the province) and the 1900 Board of Trade Building, is one of the most attractive public spaces in the country.

Victoria's streets were not always so polite or peaceful. Originally a Hudson's Bay Company fort and eventually a colonial capital, the town was a wild west scene of boardwalks, bars, muddy streets and false-fronted hotels during the 1858 gold rush. Residents were agast at the "habitual drunkenness and disgusting language" and the "houses of ill-fame" that accompanied gold fever to Victoria. Chinatown developed at this time and, until Vancouver began to grow, it was the most populous north of San Francisco. To outsiders, its alleyways were an exotic, mysterious labyrinth. Add to this a Royal Navy base, seaborne trade, cosmopolitan immigration and a local Indian reserve, and it's not surprising that Victoria's most imposing building at the time was the local jail.

At the end of the gold rush, colonial administration and civic pride put an end to this raucous period and the city rose to its bourgeois, *fin de siècle* apogee. But Vancouver became Canada's Pacific coast metropolis, leaving Victoria with its civil servants, tourists and history — and a corps of retired British colonial officials lured to the city by its well-publicized, slightly absurd English pretensions and Scottish coastal scenery. As early as 1904 the local tourist association was promoting the city as an "outpost of Empire," a phrase with a powerful resonance of loss and isolation not intended at the time. Even in the polished Belle

Epoque salons of the Empress Hotel there is that lingering melancholy of imagined lives and time gone by not entirely eclipsed by recent restoration.

At Victoria's new Eaton Centre, completed in 1990, there is no sense of imagined lives or time gone by, despite Toronto developer Cadillac Fairview's strenuous attempt to recreate the past. The centre, bounded by Government, View, Fort and Douglas streets in the centre of the historic old town, was the most controversial recent development issue in a city where change has traditionally been as leisurely as afternoon tea at the Empress Hotel. Cadillac Fairview's proposal, to rearange the furniture by redeveloping two adjacent blocks of heritage buildings in the heart of the city for a shopping mall, put the issues of growth and heritage preservation, and questions of how to manage both, at the top of the city's agenda.

The developers faced a sustained barrage of criticism from councillors, planners, thousands of concerned citizens and even local businesses over their plan to demolish ten heritage buildings to make way for a $100-million "heritage style" shopping centre. Supporters claimed that the scheme would revitalize a city centre too dependent on tourism and benefit all businesses in the vicinity by luring local shoppers away from suburban malls and into the downtown. Opponents said that the development was too large, that it would ruin the nineteenth-century character of the district, force small retailers out of business and threaten other historic buildings with the pressure for further development that the Eaton Centre's presence would be bound to attract.

Few people disputed the need for some redevelopment on the site. It is the way in which this has been achieved,

MILNE

Café Bistingo
Café Bistingo
OLD TOWNE NEWS
560
OLD TOWNE NEWS
ICE CREAM
560
La Cache
MARKET SQUARE

especially in its relationship to the city's surrounding architectural heritage and the way the old buildings on site were treated, that provoked the most vocal debate. Opponents of the original design fought a rearguard action to wrestle concessions from the developer, and Cadillac Fairview were paid by the city to retain four of the original ten heritage facades — in order, it was hoped, to preserve something of the original streetscapes amid the developer's planned heritage pastiche. The result of this compromise weakens the composition of the new design and leaves the old buildings — what's left of them — in a spatial limbo.

Given the sensitive nature of the site, the developers anticipated criticism and commissioned a building that would "fit in," rather than a bold modern design. Looking at what's been built, the latter might have been a better choice. The Eaton Centre's architects sought to use the language of nineteenth-century retail architecture in order to blend into the genuine nineteenth-century surroundings by designing a traditional-looking department store facade on Government Street and a grand arcade leading to Douglas Street. But somehow, the Belle Epoque carriage trade architecture they were copying was lost along the way. To enter the Eaton Centre is to plunge into a world of kitsch.

Here we have Georgian London, Victorian Leeds, the Crystal Palace and the Empire Exhibition of 1851, and the monumental gallerias of nineteenth-century Italy all rolled into one, with none of the intimacy one finds in modest Victorian arcades — a type which would have been more at home in Victoria's small-scale setting. In place of restrained historic re-creation (itself a questionable idea), here we have banal exploitation. There are busts of Julius Caesar, baroque cartouches, Doric columns, dolphin foun-

tains, gargoyles, Greek pediments, baronial chandeliers and contorted fairytale roof lines. And there is the "British Empire Clock," designed in French Second Empire style, which tells cosmopolitan consumers the time in Halifax, Nova Scotia, Bombay, Singapore, Brisbane, Nassau, Kowloon, London and Zanzibar — as well as playing the chimes of Big Ben. Stuck onto this appalling concoction are the four reconstituted heritage facades, their meaning as works of architecture totally removed. The Driard Hotel at View and Broad streets is a shadow of its former self. The once-delightful two-storey Victorian brick building (c. 1880) at the corner of Fort and Broad streets has been traduced by the addition of a heavy-handed chateau-style roof. In a travesty of heritage preservation, the city flattered Cadillac Fairview by declaring these pathetic remains "heritage buildings," and pasted little plaques to their facades to say so.

Criticizing the Eaton Centre by applying high standards may seem unfair. But the Eaton Centre is in the heart of one of the most precious historic areas in the country. The quality of the existing heritage buildings and the ambience of the old town demanded more sensitive and imaginative treatment than it received from Cadillac Fairview and their architects. The highest standards of commercial design were applied to the great European *fin de siècle* department stores and arcades that the Eaton Centre seeks to emulate. The glorious tiled food halls and terra-cotta facade of Harrod's in London, the stained glass dome in the Galeries Lafayette in Paris, the magnificent Galleria Vittorio Emanuele in Milan, and other examples still stand as reminders of a time when developers and retailers thought nothing of hiring the best architects and craftsmen to design and decorate their buildings. That these standards can still be achieved has actually been demonstrated in Vancouver at the Sinclair Centre, and in Victoria — in the restoration of the Parliament Buildings, the Empress Hotel and the Munro's Books building to name a few prominent examples. At the Empress one can also see new construction successfully blended with the old where the recent conference centre, whose steel and glass arcade backs onto the hotel, has been built with respectful ingenuity.

Some aspects of the Eaton Centre work sufficiently well to show what might have been achieved — but only from a distance. The main building on Government Street, in high Victorian style copied from the dismantled and partly rebuilt Driard Hotel, reinforces the street's picturesque urban character. Its rather chateau-style roof pavilions and Victorian facade seem appropriate to the city. But if you look closely at the brick veneer you can't help noticing that everything about this building — from the facade proportions, to the failure to relate the elevation to the interior floors, to the brickwork's uniform colour — is, by historic architectural standards, completely wrong. There is a further violation of architectural logic and tradition: the arcade, which should have been punched through the Government Street facade with a grand entrance consistent with the scale of the project, has been located at the Douglas Street end of the site where it fails to make an impression. The Douglas Street facade, which cries out for a four- or six-storey building, instead is a two-storey bogus heritage design whose draftsman would have won no prizes at the Ecole des Beaux Arts.

A more modest sequence of arcades could have roofed over Broad Street and penetrated the original heritage buildings, which could have been retained. Such an articulation of public space would have blended formal arcade promenades with the intangibles of surprise and serendipity, arranged on a human scale in keeping with Victoria's old town. If complete buildings could not have been retained then the heritage facades could have been kept as free-standing screens, exposed like ruins, behind which a modern steel and glass or bold concrete galleria could have sprung. But the visual metaphors and references to the past by which architects can reinterpret such heritage sites and invest them with meaning beyond their change of use, appear to have been beyond the ken of the developers and their architects. Instead, every aspect of the Eaton Centre has been designed to maximize the developer's financial return.

One ironic result of the Eaton Centre controversy has been to raise the issue of heritage preservation and increase support for this cause. Victoria does have a positive and progressive attitude toward its architectural heritage, which makes the Eaton Centre fiasco even more of an aberration. The city's comprehensive heritage management plan includes a heritage building incentive program for commercial and residential buildings that encourages owners to apply for heritage designation and helps fund maintenance and restoration. Some funding for this scheme, again not without irony, came from compensation the Eaton Centre's developers paid to the city for being allowed to close off Broad Street. What the scheme has revealed is the need for a well-informed and architecturally literate assessment of development — for local councils, planners and citizens to have the courage to say, "This is not what we want here."

When William Cornelius Van Horne, the rambunctious American general manager of the Canadian Pacific Railway, sought in the 1880s to increase traffic on the newly completed transcontinental line, he declared: "Since we can't export the scenery, we'll have to import the tourists!" He then set about building a chain of railway hotels designed to make the rail journey across Canada tolerable for well-heeled Victorian aristocrats and adventurers. In the hotels' heyday, when maps of the world blushed with the pink of the British Empire, these "icons of Canadiana" were watering holes on the imperial "all red route" from Great Britain to the colonies of Asia. They are still resonant of those days of *soignée* travel and establishment privilege — a former way of life often sentimentally displayed in sepia photographs and Victorian paintings in their opulent halls.

Whether in the wilderness or in the cities — and every Canadian city worth its salt boasts a chateauesque railway hotel like the Empress in Victoria or the Hotel Vancouver — the buildings represent an old-fashioned Canada of late Victorian European cultivation. At the Banff Springs Hotel (right) and the Chateau Lake Louise, opened as small chalet-style buildings in 1888 and 1890 respectively and extensively rebuilt and enlarged over the years, the CPR imported Swiss mountain guides and Scottish pipers to make the guests feel at home. "The finest hotel on the North American continent . . . fit for the richest Highland chieftains" was how Van Horne described the Banff Springs, a wonderful ersatz baronial castle which still stands in romantic isolation in the Rocky Mountains.

There was a noble grandeur to the giant typography above the old Canadian National Station, off Main Street south of Chinatown, in Vancouver. CANADIAN NATIONAL, spelt out in huge capital letters erected in 1928, referred not just to the Canadian National Railway (the first owner of the building) but also, in the size and confidence of the lettering, to the nation-building spirit of the age: the station was built in 1917–19 as the western terminus of Canada's second transcontinental railway, originally the Canadian Northern Pacific Railway.

The CN sign was a powerful reminder of Canada's idealistic sense of itself, a country linked from sea to sea by two transcontinental railways. The station's typography and Beaux Arts facade are evocative of noble enterprise. Few buildings in the country employed the combination of lettering and architecture — a tradition that can be traced back to Roman times — to such memorable effect. Even Vancouver's other surviving transcontinental terminus, the Canadian Pacific Railway station, completed in 1914 at the foot of Seymour Street in the city centre, and whose name is carved on the entablature above the building's colonnade, never had a sign that matched the typographic grandeur of the CNR.

Both stations have been restored for new uses: the CPR in 1976–78 for Skytrain and Seabus transit, office and retail space; the CNR in 1992–93 as a joint bus and train station. The CPR station's significant heritage features — a neoclassical facade dignified by a splendid Ionic colonnade, and a luminous booking hall decorated with salon-style paintings of the scenery through which the trains first passed in 1886 — were restored during conversion. The CNR station too has been rehabilitated with much of the original character preserved. Some of the new interior fittings veer toward pastiche, but outside, the modern addition of a high-tech-style bus bay canopy is a well-chosen contrast to the original building. With a potential high-speed train service to Seattle being mooted, and the existing VIA Rail (federal passenger railway company) transcontinental trains, long distance bus services, and local metro (Skytrain) and city bus stops nearby, the old station is being given new life as a modern transportation centre.

Controversially, though, the Canadian National sign was replaced by a facsimile bearing the moniker PACIFIC CENTRAL, the result of a competition for a new name to reflect the station's change of use — and the failure by city councillors to support their own preservation policy. The building itself and the CN sign, made locally by Neon Products, had been designated by the city in 1980. Even the Federal Heritage Railway Station Protection Act referred to the sign's "long association with the building" and said it should be retained. The fact that it was to be substituted by Pacific Central, along with a rediscovered Canadian Northern Pacific Railway title above the entrance, left heritage preservationists depressed by the city's inconsistent application of its heritage designation policy. While the new Pacific Central sign may inherit Canadian National's heritage designation, it will have none of the latter's potency and historic meaning.

PORT TOWNSEND, WASHINGTON
Jefferson County Courthouse

On his famous voyage of exploration up the West Coast in 1792, Captain George Vancouver noted Port Townsend's "safe and capacious harbour," strategically located at the entrance to Puget Sound. Vancouver sailed north and, as explorers of the time were wont to do, left in his wake the name of an aristocratic friend, the Marquis of Townshend (history has lost the "h" in the spelling) as a reminder of his presence.

Port Townsend, Washington was settled in the 1850s and given a boost when US Customs designated it the port of entry to Puget Sound. Had history shone a different light, the town might well have rivalled Vancouver or Seattle as a Pacific port. Instead it became the setting for a classic boom-and-bust tale which left the town bankrupt — but with a remarkable legacy of Victorian architecture.

Between 1888 and 1890, investors and speculators, anticipating a transcontinental railway terminus and a port on America's northern Pacific coast, began building a Victorian city at Port Townsend which, it was anticipated, would become the San Francisco of the northwest. Port Townsend became a "City of Dreams," as one local guidebook calls it — and that's how it stayed. In November 1890 the railway company, which was to connect the port with the existing Seattle and Tacoma railheads, went bust. By 1893 so had four of the town's banks. Streetcar operators pulled up their tracks, and the population fell from 7000 to 2000. Port Townsend, its main street lined with Victorian Italianate facades as rich in vanished optimism as they are in eclectic decor, became the most elaborate ghost town on the continent.

On the plateau overlooking the town and Puget Sound stands the finest monument to Port Townsend's past and fleeting glory. Surrounded, but hardly overpowered, by a suburb of gingerbread Victorian homes and later bungalows on wide, deserted streets planned for much more activity that they see today, is the magnificent Jefferson County Courthouse, completed in 1892. Seattle architect W. A. Ritchie, armed with a correspondence course in architecture from the US Treasury Department and a natural gift for picturesque composition, designed this building in the Richardsonian Romanesque style then favoured for public buildings in North America. Built to a scale befitting the town's and county's ambitions at the time, the building is still in use. It is, like the town, well preserved as part of a US national historic district. With its stout stonework and brick facades laced with ornamental details, and its lofty campanile, it is a near-perfect expression of Victorian public virtue and self-regard: "What boom, what bust?" it seems to say. "Just look at what we could build in those days!"

The Cariboo gold rush of 1858 lured many Chinese to British Columbia from Hong Kong and San Francisco. They worked as miners and camp followers in the shanty towns and gold fields of the interior or settled in Victoria and, later, Vancouver. Vancouver's Chinatown grew after the Canadian Pacific Railway brought in 10,000 labourers from China to help build the railway up the Fraser Canyon, following the route of the Cariboo gold rush road built by the Royal Engineers. Vancouver's Chinese worked as cooks in hotels, logging camps and mills, ran laundries, import businesses, small farms and, infamously, opium dens around Vancouver's Shanghai Alley, across from where the Chinese Freemasons Building (below) now stands.

Many Chinatown buildings in Vancouver and Victoria are an eclectic blend of east and west, with facades variously adorned with classical columns, cornices, Cantonese lettering and Chinese recessed balconies, stirred together in a likable hodge-podge. At Lee's Benevolent Association (right), built in 1911 at 614 Fisgard Street in Victoria, Romanesque arches frame the recessed balconies. The Chinese Freemasons Building in Vancouver, built around 1901 at the corner of Pender and Carrall streets, is unusual in that it clearly separates eastern and western styles. The Pender Street facade sports the recessed balconies typical of Chinatown architecture, and a traditional way of building in the port cities of the South China Sea, the homeland of most early Chinese immigrants to British Columbia. The Carrall Street facade, however, is Victorian, slightly Italianate, in style. It acknowledges the European character of that street: a block north, the Hastings and Carrall corner was the centre of Vancouver's early Edwardian downtown.

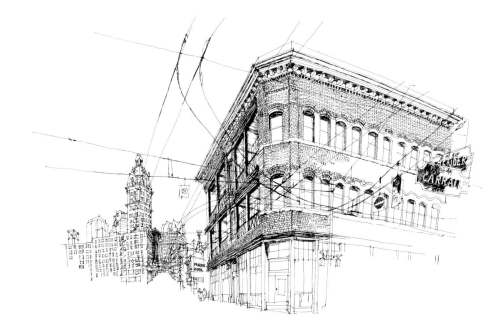

THE LEES BENEVOLENT ASSOCIATION

鄧友會義崇成鉄

行華園芳春興宏
FUNG HING HONG Co. CHINESE HERBS

富贵歸飲店
FORUM CHINESE RESTAURANT

LAW
OFFICE

LEE
ASSOCIATION
614

612 FISCHARD

614
FUNG HING
HONG

P EACH
TWO
DOLLARS
$125

1903

Gladiola
Bethens

The New World Hotel, built at the corner of Powell and Dunlevy streets in Vancouver's Downtown Eastside, was once known as the Tamura Building, named after the Japanese businessman who built it in 1912–13. It has cultural as well as architectural significance, as Powell Street was the centre of Vancouver's Japantown before the population was interned during World War Two. When a new owner appeared recently, the building was in an appalling state of disrepair. The ornamental Corinthian columns and bracketed cornice were rusting away, bits of the building were falling onto the sidewalk, and one of the Corinthian capitals had been removed. Faced with an order from the city's Department of Permits and Licences to make the building safe, the owner elected to restore the New World Hotel rather than strip it of all the fanciful but collapsing decoration. A less sensitive owner would have taken the latter course which would have robbed the structure of its heritage value.

The brickwork and the ground floor granite were steam-cleaned, but it was found that much of the original ornamental metalwork was beyond repair, especially the fluted corner Corinthian columns and elaborate cornice that lend the hotel the incongruous character of a plantation mansion in Virginia. A local artist was commissioned to recast pieces of the classical columns in fibreglass, while architect Robert Lemon worked out the period colour scheme after taking paint samples from the dismantled, rusting ornament. Unfortunately it was not possible to reinstate the building's original sash windows. If the city gave grants, as Victoria does, to encourage full and faithful restoration of heritage buildings, this work might have been done — and more heritage building owners might be persuaded to follow suit.

The New World Hotel's proprietor received a City of Vancouver heritage award in 1992 for his efforts. The well-established and wide-ranging heritage award scheme recognizes successful restoration and adaptive reuse of heritage buildings, compatible new design, engineering and craft techniques in restoration, and community efforts, among other things, and generally promotes a climate in which preservation is seen as a positive alternative to demolition.

The city also has a Heritage Conservation Foundation, a non-profit society charged with receiving donations and property, giving grants for heritage preservation and encouraging related activities. It was launched in 1992 with the gift of Glen Brae to Vancouver. How consistent the foundation's funding and performance will be is unclear in a city which at times seems unable to stand firm when major issues, the fate of the Canadian National sign, for example, have to be dealt with.

The Dr. Sun Yat-Sen Garden in Vancouver's Chinatown appears to western eyes as a quaint miniature landscape of tangled foliage, twisted trees and rocky grotesquerie around an artificial pond enclosed by white walls and tiled roofs—a seemingly indecipherable maze. "Everything has a place and a meaning," a guide tells visitors before they begin to walk over the little bridges, along the angled corridors and inside the carved pavilions.

There are three types of Chinese garden: imperial gardens, monastery gardens and smaller, usually urban gardens for scholars and the gentry. While the casual visitor will only see what seems a blue willow china pattern brought to life, the guide explains every nuance and detail of the Sun Yat-Sen garden's design—and, should you mention it, that it owes nothing to the willow pattern, which was inspired by Chinese scenes but originated in eighteenth-century England. The Sun Yat-Sen classical garden recreates a scholar's garden of the Ming period (1368–1644). The garden (not to be mistaken for the public park directly east) is situated behind the Chinese Cultural Centre at Carrall and Pender streets, and it is the only full-size classical Chinese garden outside China. Completed by architect Joe Wai in 1986 and based on examples in the city of Suzhou, it was the result of local initiative, diplomacy and traditional craftsmanship. Artisans from Suzhou built the garden by hand, using traditional techniques and materials from China.

It occurred to me as I drew this oasis of limestone, exquisite pavilions and jade waters that few people in the West could re-create, say, an Italian Renaissance garden with quite the same conviction and authority. Western architects and designers, driven by a relentless desire for novelty, tend to refer to the past only in the most meretricious of ways. We don't build real Greek or Roman columns; we build badly proportioned cheap fakes. But the designers of the Sun-Yat-Sen garden clearly value continuity. Quiet retreats like this one, reflecting a quest for symbolic harmony with the natural and spiritual worlds, achieved perfect expression centuries ago.

The garden commemorates Dr. Sun Yat-Sen (1866–1925), who is known as the father of modern China. In 1905 he founded the Chinese United Party, which became the Kuomintang (Chinese Nationalist League). He visited Vancouver twice during his international campaign to overthrow the Manchu dynasty (abolished in the revolution of 1911) and establish a democratic Chinese republic. Chinese Canadians across the country contributed to his cause and financed the league's western Canada headquarters, built in 1920 and still standing at the corner of Pender and Gore streets. W. E. Sproat, an immigrant Scottish architect, played safe with his unusual client and designed the Chinese Nationalist League building in turn-of-the-century commercial style, but added a pagoda-style turret at the corner. The turret has long been removed but the Kuomintang still own the building. Upstairs in antiquated offices, a hand-coloured photograph of an ageless Sun Yat-Sen presides over chain-smoking officials who still hold regular meetings here.

LORD STRATHCONA SCHOOL
Headmaster's House

Lord Strathcona School was named after the Scottish-born director of the Canadian Pacific Railway. Its origin goes back to the earliest days of immigrant settlement in Vancouver—to the original fifteen children of the Hastings Mill community who studied in a little clapboard schoolhouse built by the mill company in 1865. The first permanent building on the present site was the East School, built in 1891. It was a handsome structure, built with bricks and granite imported from Britain, apparently as ship's ballast. The East School survived until 1920 when it was dismantled, but its bricks and granite were recycled and can still be seen in the Primary Building facing East Pender Street. The building's French Second Empire tower, unfortunately, was not reused. A larger block was built in 1897 on Keefer Street (left) and this is now the oldest public school building in Vancouver.

Expansion of the school was largely a result of the growth that followed the arrival of the CPR in Vancouver in 1886. "The school of many nations" reflects Vancouver's ethnic diversity—children of Chinese, Japanese, Russian, Ukrainian, Italian, Portuguese, Scottish, Irish and other origins. Architect William Blackmore designed the block shown here, originally with a chateauesque central tower and heavily balustraded outside stairs, long since removed. He set his school building on a foundation of rusticated Romanesque granite, visually expressing the educational foundation pupils at Strathcona have received for more than a hundred years.

Across the street from the school is a picturesque, turreted old home with a faceted entrance framed by gables decorated with delicate gingerbread trim. This whimsical Queen Anne house (below), prominent on its corner at 602 Keefer Street, is one of the most notable in the Strathcona neighbourhood, and not only for its distinctive composition. The home was built for Gregory Thom, a headmaster of Lord Strathcona School. Thom is said to have had his office in the turret, from which vantage point he could keep an eye on his school across the street. The house, which dates from around 1902, has recently been restored by a new owner. Reroofing, so often completed in a manner that is incompatible with heritage homes, here has been sympathetically done with a pattern that imitates the original shingles. The original Edwardian colour scheme, now vividly and daringly painted over, is anyone's guess. But in form, detail and spirit, the home has retained its period character. The porch, previously enclosed by boards and partitions, has been opened up to form a delightful columned space from where, like headmaster Thom in his turret, the owner can sit and watch the schoolchildren at play.

BALLANTYNE PIER
Versatile Pacific Shipyard

Ballantyne Pier, with its four impressive storage sheds with concrete-columned interiors, was built at the north foot of Heatley Street in Vancouver in 1923. What made the pier exceptional, though, were the four facades that acted as bookends to the sheds. Built in brick and concrete, the concrete fashioned as stone quoins and keystones, the facades were truly monumental in scale. To walk down to the north end of the pier and suddenly encounter the two seaward facades (one of which is shown here) was to encounter a vision of the majestic architecture of the industrial revolution. Unfortunately, all the facades had been allowed to deteriorate and were in poor condition by 1991 when the Vancouver Port Corporation proposed redevelopment. Ballantyne Pier was to become a "modern, multi-use terminal combining cruise-passenger and general-cargo handling facilities (wood pulp) while retaining heritage features of the old structure."

The interior space, however, did not permit the movement that modern cargo handling requires: three sheds and part of the fourth have been demolished. Three of the heritage facades were also torn down, as repairs were deemed too expensive. The remaining facade and part of its shed, at the southeast corner of the pier, have been retained and renovated as a cruise ship passenger terminal. This surviving facade, with its 1920s aura, will make a fitting cruise ship facility, but the paired facades which gave Ballantyne Pier its special character have vanished forever.

Perhaps all this would have been acceptable if the new facility promised to be as eye-catching and aesthetically pleasing as the heritage buildings it was to replace. But the port's initial proposal was for a dull, if functional, new shed at the landward end of the pier, disguised in a mock-Georgian style intended to "fit in" with the surviving heritage facade. Even worse was the idea—still not abandoned—to replicate the demolished seaward facades and stick imitations on to the new storage shed—the worst of both worlds. Heritage preservation is not accomplished by replicating facades, nor is it achieved by demolishing three out of four original elevations.

Nobody was suggesting that the port build a Sydney Opera House on Ballantyne Pier, but critics of the scheme thought that with a bit of imagination and structural ingenuity, and the desire to wave the flag for the city and the port, a memorable modern building could be constructed. To its credit, the port corporation continued to seek public and professional opinion on the matter—something it is not obliged to do—and has redesigned its new building in high-tech nautical style, potentially a vigorous contrast to the surviving heritage facade.

As a Glaswegian, I found a depressing familiarity in the news in late 1991 that the Versatile Pacific Shipyard on Vancouver's North Shore was to close. Glasgow was once the foremost shipbuilding centre in the world. Close to a third of the world's steamships were built on the River Clyde in Edwardian times. But today, apart from memories and model ships in the local transport museum, virtually nothing remains of this proud industry. After World War Two foreign competition, mismanagement and an inflexible labour force launched, not ships, but an irreversible decline. Vancouver's shipyards never produced anything like the Clyde-built Queen Mary, but that same muscular craftsmanship and pride did flourish here at one time. Versatile Pacific had not quite lived up to its name in later years, but the yard was not without tradition.

The shipyard was founded in 1906 by Alfred Wallace, a shipwright's son from Brixham, the fishing port in Devon, England. Wallace began building ships on False Creek in 1894, then moved to the North Shore where his shipyard grew to become the biggest in BC. It remained in the family as a legacy of Victorian industrial enterprise until 1971. In its heyday during World War Two, the Wallace Shipyard (by then known as the Burrard Dry Dock company) was a focus for the local community, employing 10,000 men and women on the North Shore and at its south Burrard yard, formerly at the foot of McLean Drive. The yards built dozens of ships for the British and Canadian merchant marine and Royal Canadian Navy. As I walked along the piers and through the empty sheds littered with rusting machinery, I felt like an explorer who has stumbled upon a vast, uninhabited relic of civilization. But then I fancied I heard the voices of those 10,000 workers, the crackle of their welding torches and the lunchtime hooters.

Beside one of the antiquated cranes I came across a faded sign by a silent slipway. It was inscribed boldly: "Versatile Pacific Shipyards Inc., Hull 110, CCGS Henry Larsen, Type 1,200 Icebreaker. Keel Laid Aug. 23, 1985. Launch Date Jan. 3, 1987." How Canadian, I thought. An icebreaker, built to patrol the Northwest Passage, a patriotic duty now abandoned. "Henry Larsen," the inscription continued, "was the master of the RCMP vessel St. Roch, built by Burrard Dry Dock in 1928." (The famous *St. Roch* sailed through the Northwest Passage and is preserved at the Vancouver Maritime Museum at Vanier Park.) Also abandoned here, along with the Polar 8 icebreaker project that would have saved the shipyard, is a way of life and a community of labour. Looking around at the creeping dilapidation I was

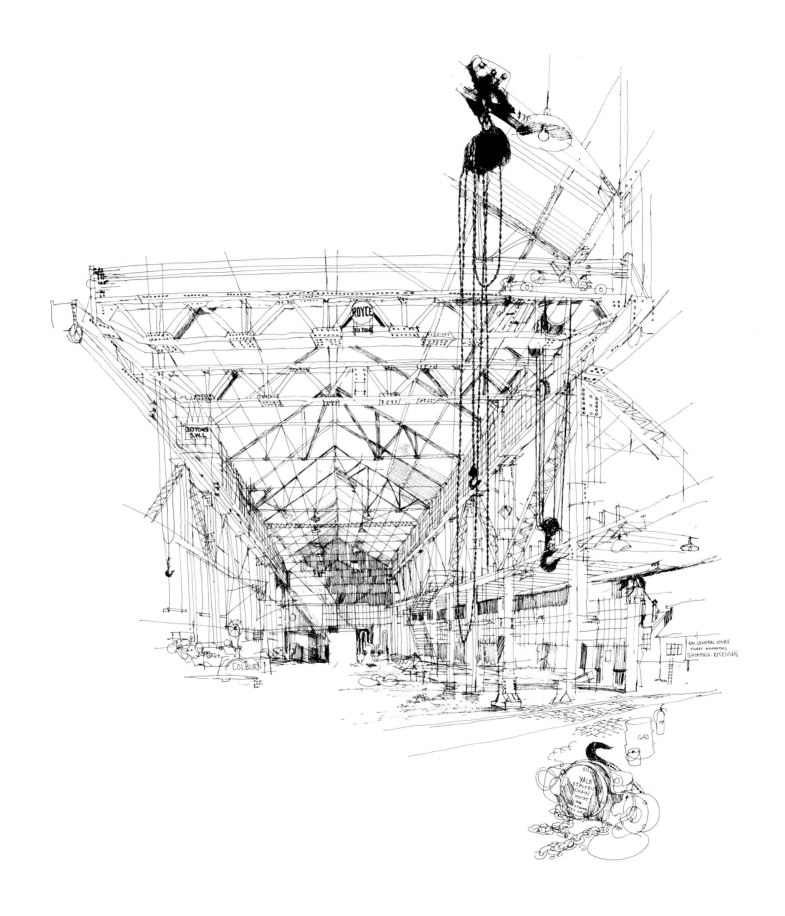

saddened at the dissipation of traditional shipbuilders' skills and the self-respect they represent.

Nobody's going to build icebreakers here any more, but the waterfront site, just east of Lonsdale Quay, does offer opportunity for creative redevelopment. Just how creative and beneficial to the local community and its displaced shipbuilders this will be remains to be seen, because here redevelopment promises to be a controversial issue. The Cates tugboat yard and a huge floating dock (a notable piece of marine architecture capable of repairing ships of up to 38,000 tons) will continue some traditional marine work close to the historic Versatile Pacific site. But it seems likely that the shipyard will be rezoned from industrial to commercial and residential use. This would please Versatile Pacific and its creditors, and developers eager to build condos on the prime waterfront property, replacing derelict industrial buildings with flashy opportunism.

But not everyone is keen to see the bulldozers roll. The City of North Vancouver recently commissioned a heritage study of the Versatile Pacific site, identifying structures that are worth saving. Lack of investment over the years has served to preserve the yard's antiquated buildings and wharves, some of which date from before World War One. Even in, or perhaps because of, its current state of abandoned preservation, the old Wallace Shipyard merits designation as a national historic site. The huge machine shop of 1925 (left) is a typical example of a forceful industrial architecture which ought to be preserved, along with the cranes and piers which give the site its identity. There is potential to adapt the shipyard in a creative way — to balance the heritage aspects with the pressure to redevelop.

Development of some kind seems unavoidable. The way it's achieved, though, will shape the North Shore waterfront for years to come. The piers, cranes and industrial buildings at the Lonsdale Quay end of the site (historically and architecturally the most significant grouping) could become the Granville Island of the North Shore — with the invigorating melange of artistic, commercial and industrial activity that implies. Public access to the waterfront and the site from Lonsdale Quay eastward, integration of the site with the Lower Lonsdale heritage district, and an overall management and design policy would be essential ingredients in the success of such a scheme.

In the longer term, the shipyard would be an ideal location for an expanded North Shore Museum close to the port activity that has been such an important aspect of the area's history and development. Small workshops and light industry could also be encouraged here to make use of the existing buildings, and sympathetically designed modern additions. The eastern half of the shipyard could be redeveloped as a high-density residential district (persuading people to live in this still-industrial area would be a precondition for success). Mixing commercial, residential and industrial uses on the same site contradicts most planners' orderly, not to say sanitized, vision of urban life. But creative rezoning and redevelopment, with Granville Island as a model, would be the best way to ensure that everyone benefits from the changes that are inevitable here.

When I first stumbled across Britannia Beach, toward the head of Howe Sound, the shifting morning fog revealed a ghost town of milky clapboard facades set in a landscape pebbled with rusting, antiquated machinery. As the swirling vapour eddied up the hillside I was astonished to see a gigantic corrugated iron structure, built as a series of stepbacks, clinging to the slope. It looked like a huge dead armadillo. The Britannia Mining and Smelting company built this creature in 1923. The concentrator, as it is known, is the most visible and spectacular relic of a mining operation which, in its heyday, was the largest producer of copper in the British Empire.

Alexander Allen Forbes, an adventurous Scot, local medical officer and part-time prospector, discovered copper deposits on the mountains above the sound in 1888. But Forbes moved on, and it wasn't until the early 1900s that the area's mineral potential began to be exploited. A townsite, still well preserved, was established at Britannia Beach. A second township (now destroyed) was built up in the mountains to service the mines, as they were being developed. Ore was shifted by narrow-gauge railway from the mines four miles inland, dumped at the top of the concentrator, and processed by a series of gravity-fed steps to sea level before being shipped down the sound.

Until the 1950s there was neither a road nor a railway to Britannia Beach. The mining community, with its church, school, clapboard houses and general store, was quite isolated, despite its proximity to Vancouver. This isolation makes the construction of the concentrator an extraordinary feat. There's a severe and single-minded purpose to this building's presence and a nineteenth-century swagger to its Empire-building stride up the mountain. Architecturally its form perfectly describes its function—to digest the ore from the mountainside on which it climbs.

There is a rich metaphorical aspect to the concentrator's beached presence in the natural beauty of Howe Sound. Rusting away on its hillside, it stands as a symbol of a greedy, polluting society as much as it is a monument to human ingenuity and the nobility of labour. The precipitous interior, once a cathedral of industrial technology, today presents a scene of tumbling dereliction. Seeing it, I thought: This is not the past, but the future. This is how cities will look when all the natural resources which sustain our profligate civilization run out.

The Britannia Beach Historical Society, which owns the concentrator, understands its historic and social significance, and perhaps its metaphorical resonance as well. The society campaigned successfully to have the property designated as a National Historic Site in 1988, followed by provincial landmark designation. Undaunted by the size and present condition of the concentrator, they operate the site as the British Columbia Museum of Mining and have ambitious plans to establish it as a model for heritage development in Canada, with a new community funded by private and public investment.

Vancouver has a long and happy association with Bowen Island. Until the late 1950s thousands of Vancouverites went there on their holidays aboard the Union Steamship Company's fleet of pleasure steamers. On summer weekends in the 1930s, downtown piers were alive with frolicking holiday-makers and day-trippers. They called Bowen the "Happy Isle." The Union Steamship Company built a resort around Snug Cove in the 1920s with a hotel, dance hall, tennis courts, picnic grounds, dozens of cottages and a general store.

Snug Cove, where the ferry from West Vancouver docks, is aptly named. It's a pleasant spot, quiet and randomly residential. But this sleepy little community is now changing as association with and proximity to the big city becomes less benign. Little remains of the original resort. The surviving cluster of charming vernacular cottages— the Orchard Cottages, a vital part of the island's heritage— and the general store are last reminders of the Union Steamship Company's holiday village. Two were recently knocked down and the others threatened with demolition to make way for an ill-considered redevelopment which would also have filled in the nearby tidal flats. Local protest fought off the attempts, and development which has gone ahead (a marina and restaurant) is less of an eyesore than was first feared, mainly because of vociferous local concern. Elsewhere on the island, though, pressure to develop is increasing as people move to Bowen, attracted by its rural charm and convenient ferry access to the city.

Still, some parts of the island remain unspoiled. The Collins Farm (left) seems not to have changed for years. The picturesque farmhouse was built for Glasgow-born James Collins, who came to Canada as a sponsored orphan and worked on a farm in New Brunswick before moving to Bowen Island around 1904. Collins cleared the land for his farm and eventually built the house in 1924. The farm is no longer worked and the house is set on a diminished, but still spacious, estate. Still in the same family, it gives a glimpse of a rural way of life that is slowly disappearing on Bowen Island. At the entrance to the farm the Bowen Island United Church, the first on the island when it was built in 1932, adds to a pleasing historic ensemble. Before the church was built, services were held in the island schoolhouse and Sunday school in residents' homes.

If you drive far enough south through well-manicured suburbs in Richmond, you'll eventually find a landscape of fields and homesteads in the mile or so before the Fraser River. It's a curious place, not without charm and still agricultural with its dykes and ditches, but too close to the city to remain entirely so for long unless land use is strictly controlled. Some of the farms now boast incongruous, sprawling monster homes next to tumbledown traditional barns, strawberry fields and vegetable patches. The surreal quality these intruders bring to the empty landscape is quite enjoyable at first sight, but the novelty soon wears off. Few of these new homes — and so far there are not many — show any sensitivity to their rural surroundings or the local vernacular architecture. Postmodern porticos look bad enough in the suburbs — but here?

This part of Richmond (where No. 3 Road meets the river) has been settled and farmed since the 1860s and several old farms suggest the architectural vocabulary by which new homes might better fit into the area. Modern homes needn't all be copies of London Farm (shown here), but if local planners were to consider design guidelines for new development on agricultural land they could do worse than refer to the scale, use of materials, landscaping and general friendly character of this traditional home. London Farm, now a municipal park site at 6511 Dyke Road, dates from the 1880s and has been restored by the Richmond Historical and Museum Society to its pre-1914 condition.

You might think there isn't much heritage in a community as young as Richmond. But beneath the surface of relentless suburban development there's an older and richer strain of life, not quite extinguished. At Steveston, a busy fishing harbour originally settled by Japanese fishermen, some late-nineteenth-century small-town ambience survives, along with the impressive century-old Gulf of Georgia Cannery, currently being restored. On the bank of the Fraser River, the Britannia Shipyard, built as the Britannia Cannery in 1889, is also being restored. This was one of the first salmon canneries on the Fraser River, and grew to be one of the largest. The Anglo–British Columbia Packing Company converted the cannery to a boatyard in 1919 and the company's fishing boats were built and repaired there until 1969. In the heyday of the BC fishing and canning industry, in the early 1900s, ABC was one of the biggest exporters of Pacific salmon, sending canned fish as far away as Europe, Asia and Australia. The Canadian Fishing Company ran the yard until it was abandoned in 1979. Now it's being rebuilt by the Britannia Heritage Shipyard Society with support from the city of Richmond. A local area plan sees the yard becoming part of a recreational and heritage trail along the Steveston waterfront from Scotch Pond to London Farm.

Elsewhere in Richmond, though, low-density suburban development threatens to consume available land. Here is a world of gated theme communities and monster homes — a flat, depressing landscape planned exclusively with car commuters in mind. Some of the winding developments, many designed in mock-Tudor style, attempt to create a village atmosphere marketed as a bit of "olde England." But where you would find shopfronts and pubs in the Cotswolds, here there is only a dismal sequence of double garage doors.

On the Terra Nova lands development, for example, a controversial rezoning of agricultural land south of the airport, all that remains of the natural world displaced are

ducks and marsh grass painted on real estate signs that bear soothing messages like: "Shaughnessy by tradition, Richmond by nature," and "A carefully designed neighbourhood by Progressive Construction." But there are no neighbourhoods in such developments. There are no shops, no proper streets and no public transport. In 1992, twenty-seven different builders were listed as being responsible for phase one of Terra Nova, with thirteen more for phase two. But many hands do not always make light work. All one finds here are more double garage doors fronting pompous monster homes, arranged cheek-by-jowl to form streetscapes of grotesque banality.

The same suburban sprawl — hugely inefficient for access to public services — disfigures much of Greater Vancouver. Terra Nova just seems worse because the site, facing the northern arm of the Fraser River, deserved more imaginative treatment. There is no reference here to the riverbank/seaside locale in either the street layout, which could have been designed to frame street-end water and mountain views, or in the architecture, which could have picked up on the clapboard idiosyncrasies and varied heights and densities of older homes or the sensitivity of the contemporary West Coast style, where landscape and architecture are sympathetically entwined.

Sadly, the ethos behind Terra Nova and similar development seems to have none of that indefinable sense of place that good design and planning can engender. I found a sign reading "Free Rocks" on the edge of the site, above a scattering of boulders the builders had dug up and could find no use for. Every square foot on the Terra Nova has been so thoroughly exploited that even the rocks are in the way.

A handful of Lower Mainland communities have, so far, escaped the relentless suburbanization which is drifting up the Fraser Valley from Vancouver. Time stopped at Clayburn, a sleepy hamlet east of the Abbotsford–Mission highway, when the brickworks closed in 1930. The Clayburn Company, once the largest producer of bricks in the province, was established after John Charles Maclure discovered seams of fire clay — used for heat-resistant bricks — on the flanks of Sumas Mountain in 1905. He built a narrow-gauge railway to move clay from the mine to the brickworks in the small company town. Maclure's brother, Samuel, who became famous as the architect of Tudor Revival villas in Edwardian Victoria and Vancouver, is said to have designed the brick houses of Clayburn that give the village its charm and distinction.

There's a varied architectural heritage in the village; old barns, wooden houses and little brick bungalows with tidy gardens caused an English visitor in the 1920s to describe the place as "a quaint English village." Clayburn Presbyterian Church, built in 1912 (right), has a Nordic/Scottish personality, although its walls are of local brick like those of the workers' bungalows, plant manager's house and general store. Many old buildings in Victoria and Vancouver (the Sun Tower, for example) once used Clayburn bricks. Nothing remains of the brickworks today; they were demolished after the plant closed when the clay seam ran out. Clayburn village declined to the point that the store was featured in a book of ghost towns of British Columbia. But the villagers, who appreciate Clayburn's significant historic and architectural value, have been working in the last few years to restore its unique heritage.

This view of Vancouver's Beatty Street is punctuated by the colossal Sun Tower, the tallest building in the British Empire when it was completed in 1912 for newspaper publishing baron Louis D. Taylor. It terminates a monumental urban streetscape lined with several fine Edwardian warehouses. There's a stout—and, on the Sun Tower, florid—quality of Victorian England to the architecture here, perhaps referring to Liverpool, a city to whose repute Vancouver aspired at the time.

Halfway down the block is the Beatty Building at 540 Beatty Street, an unusual work by architects Somervell & Putnam, who were better known for their elaborate Greco/Roman banks. The building is one of the finest warehouses of its period in the city. Number 550 is an infill design by Bruno Freschi which manages some individuality and confidence while being sympathetic to its neighbours' Edwardian classicism. The Pendera on Pender Street, built in 1990 at the foot of Beatty Street for the Downtown Eastside Residents Association, is also a good example of sensitivity to heritage surroundings.

The lively urban quality of this block has influenced the planning of the nearby "International Village" currently being developed, initially by Concord Pacific. A huge, mixed-use redevelopment bounded by Pender, Beatty and Chinatown, it promises to echo the energetic traditional streetscape shown here—a welcome change from the clichéd tower-and-plaza concept normally favoured for such projects. Too few developers, architects and planners know how to patch up the urban texture with respect to existing surroundings, but here, the scale and density of the neighbouring heritage buildings seems to have been a positive inspiration for the adjacent new project.

Vancouver's late nineteenth-century plutocrats had names which sounded as grand as their enterprises. Benjamin Tingley Rogers arrived in Vancouver from New York and established Canada's first sugar refinery in the city in 1890. He gained the confidence of the Canadian Pacific Railway and the budding city of Vancouver and was granted tax concessions for his business, which helped develop the port of Vancouver.

Rogers Sugar went on to become a province-wide conglomerate which owned plantations in Fiji and Cuba, and as BC Sugar it is still a well-known brand name today. B. T. Rogers profited sufficiently from his enterprise to build two of Vancouver's best-known heritage homes — the Gabriola in the West End, and the palatial Shannon on Granville Street at 57th Avenue.

Less known but just as important historically are the industrial buildings which Rogers built to found his empire. The most notable of these still stands near the docks at 123 Rogers Street, easily seen from Powell Street. Built in 1902 as the Refined Sugar Warehouse, the spectacular brick building is reminiscent of the best British industrial architecture of the nineteenth century. When I first stumbled across this monumental structure, it reminded me of the grand, now decaying Victorian Italianate textile mills of Lancashire and Yorkshire in England. Few of Vancouver's port buildings speak of this sort of industrial glory and enterprise. The massive grain elevators of the 1920s certainly do and, until its demolition, so did nearby Ballantyne Pier. Rogers' Refined Sugar Warehouse is now the best surviving industrial building of its era in the city.

When built in 1897 for the Hudson's Bay Company, this was the tallest building in Vancouver. More impressive today is its strongly composed Richardsonian Romanesque elevation executed in the robust style popular at the time. The style was named after H. H. Richardson, the American architect who revived and reinterpreted the European Romanesque style of the Middle Ages in nineteenth-century America. Richardson worked mainly in Boston and Chicago in the 1870s and 1880s, but his style, characterized by heavily chiselled stonework, medieval carving, cavernous arched entrances and rhythmic arched windows, became well travelled as the railways and frontier settlements (for which the style seemed vigorously suited) crossed and mapped the continent. Canada's best-known Richardsonian Romanesque buildings include Windsor Station, Montreal, built in 1887–89, and Toronto's old City Hall, 1889–99. The Hudson's Bay warehouse at 321 Water Street is not in the same league, but it is the most elegant example of the style in Vancouver.

The rhythmic facade of Hudson House is derived from ancient Roman and later Romanesque buildings—influences that have reappeared with an unexpected postmodern twist in the controversial plans for the new Vancouver Public Library building. The design that won the 1992 Library Square architectural competition stunned citizens when it was unveiled—it looked like the Colosseum in Rome. The winning team of architects, Moshe Safdie and Downs–Archambault, were reportedly amused that the public confused their design with the ancient Roman arena.

When it is done well, postmodern architecture can reinterpret the past in new ways—much as H. H. Richardson

did in the nineteenth century, but with more freedom and humour. Library Square promises to be a flamboyant and entertaining example of this approach to architecture. The trouble with postmodernism, though, is that it can degenerate into vulgarity and meaningless historicism—a sort of billboard architecture for every two-bit developer trying to sell you a condo. Architects in the past were, as part of their training, required to study and make measured drawings of classical buildings to learn the language of proportion and detail that was established by the builders of ancient Greece and Rome. Postmodern design rarely shows this discipline and sensitivity.

The selection of the colosseum design over a complex modernist entry was justified in part by the thought that the building refers to sources of knowledge and Western civilization. A copy of the Parthenon would have been a more accurate choice in this respect: cultural reference and symbolism are important aspects of architecture, but they imply knowledge of and respect for the past that can give meaning to the future. There seems little of the future in Library Square's outward appearance, and respect for the past may not be achieved by sticking bits of faux classical detail on the library facade, as shown on the model of the winning design. What Library Square does have are some spectacular and potentially popular public spaces that may save Vancouver the embarrassment of having its major contemporary public building viewed in future as a monumental folly. And if Library Square can be executed with a more abstract sensitivity to the forms and proportion of the classical architecture it symbolically emulates, then the city may end up with a landmark library building which will be more than just a tourist attraction.

Vancouver's examples of the Richardsonian Romanesque style, found mainly in Gastown, are impressive enough, but to see the real McCoy you have to go to the Pioneer Square historic district of Seattle. Pioneer Square has much in common with Gastown. Both are old commercial districts which boomed after the railways arrived and during the Klondike gold rush. Both became Skid Road areas and were threatened by 1960s urban "renewal" — of the sort achieved with bulldozers and expressways. Fortunately both escaped this bleak fate and have been somewhat revived, initially as tourist attractions but, increasingly, by being diversified with offices and residences sympathetic to their historic surroundings. Where the districts differ is in their architecture. While Seattle experienced the same boom-and-bust cycles as Vancouver in the late nineteenth century, it always emerged a step ahead of its Canadian rival. In 1897, for example, when the SS *Portland* sailed into Seattle with the first shipment of Klondike gold, the city became the main departure point for the Yukon, gaining a head start over Vancouver and Victoria.

Gastown's major buildings date from this time, but Pioneer Square was already well established. There is nothing in Vancouver to compare with the Pioneer Building (left), a magnificent Richardsonian Romanesque structure designed with blowsy confidence by Elmer Fisher, a Massachusetts architect clearly familiar with the master's work. In 1892 when it was completed, the American Institute of Architects called it "the finest building west of Chicago." Inside the building, restored in the 1970s, there are two galleried atriums, and (unusual survivors) the original open cage elevators.

In its architecture, Victory Square is one of the most evocative Edwardian public spaces in Canada. All around the sloping square are the relics of old empires—the Dominion Building (shown here), the tallest in the British Empire when completed in 1910, the Daily Province Building and the Sun Tower, and Woodward's department store. This old downtown district, with its marble lobbies and Beaux Arts stonework, declined as the city centre moved west, and has remained largely unchanged. This is also where the CPR's Scottish surveyor, Lauchlan Alexander Hamilton, staked out the grid of the future metropolis—in 1885, in what was then "the silent solitude of the primeval forest," according to a commemorative plaque at Hastings and Hamilton streets. The shape of Victory Square (actually not square) is a result of Hamilton's work: a new alignment of streets colliding with the older Gastown grid.

The Dominion Building, with its Parisian-style mansard roof, lavish terra-cotta veneer, and titanic Roman entrance columns, is better maintained than other buildings in the area. Farther down Hastings Street the Edwardian facades present a picture of crumbling decay—exacerbated in 1993 by the closure of the long-established Woodward's store. This was once the flagship of one of the most extensive retail chains in western Canada, and the rooftop sign, a miniature Eiffel Tower with a huge *W* at the top, is a local landmark.

The oldest building on the present Woodward's site (the first store was opened in 1883 at Main and Georgia) dates from 1908. This was swallowed up over the years by numerous extensions, but you can still see the original facades at the corner of Hastings and Abbott. These, if not the whole building, should be preserved if the site is redeveloped. The worst possible outcome of Woodward's closure would be to leave the building boarded up. Hastings Street does not need any more abandoned heritage buildings. What it does need are decent homes for local and new residents, jobs, and small- to medium-sized businesses. Converting Woodward's to mixed social and commercial use (as recently proposed by the Downtown Eastside Residents Association) could arrest the area's decline. City planners have identified the Hastings Street corridor through Victory Square as a potential heritage area to be administered with guidelines for appropriate development. Its Edwardian streetscape, extending from the Marine Building all the way past Main Street, is remarkable for its consistency and character. Preserving the area while encouraging the diversity and density that will make revitalization and architectural conservation work, is the challenge to be met.

Community groups are concerned that pressure for development may overtake the city Planning Department's good intentions. Victory Square's historic buildings will be vulnerable to change as the district is steered out of the doldrums. Should new buildings here be allowed to share the streetscape with the old? Should they look new (if the design quality is good enough perhaps they should) or should they look old (clad in ersatz Edwardian fancy dress)? How many historic facades should be kept, and to what extent should complete buildings be retained? DERA's Woodward's proposal—and another DERA idea to redevelop heritage buildings directly across Hastings Street from Woodward's, with new construction prominent behind partly retained facades—have been stymied by a lack of funding. But their initiatives do grapple with the crucial questions, setting the architectural agenda for Victory Square's future development and revival.

Between 1909 and 1919, forty-two warehouses were built in Vancouver's Yaletown, close to the CPR freight yards which once covered the land between False Creek and what is now Pacific Boulevard. Most still stand, their facades giving the 1000–1200 blocks of Homer, Hamilton and Mainland streets a consistent heritage character. Generally four or five storeys tall and built with heavy timber or concrete structural frames, expressed on the facades by generously glazed, gridlike fenestration, some of the buildings here seem quite modern in their rhythm. Decoration, less evident than on earlier Gastown warehouses, is confined to entrance and cornice details if there is any at all. At 1090 Homer Street, the rusticated ground floor stone piers and brick facade, rising to a corbelled brick (often terra-cotta) cornice, are typical features of the Edwardian commercial style common to both office buildings and warehouses. 1090 Homer's rear facade, however, is spare and unadorned.

With the postwar decline in local rail distribution, and the removal of the railway yards in the 1970s, Yaletown seemed destined for demolition or, at best, creeping dilapidation. But the solidly built old warehouses offered spacious premises for artists, architects and small businesses, and the run-down industrial buildings offered character and (initially) low rents. Today many of the district's old buildings have been renovated in a process of preservation and renewal — some would call it gentrification (the area's crude but vigorous painted company signs that decorated the area's buildings have been mostly scrubbed away). But developers have been encouraged to retain existing facades, preserving the area's period streetscapes and the old railway loading bays on Hamilton and Mainland streets.

The original loading bay canopies have fared less well. Some have been removed and others are deteriorating — unfortunate, because the canopies are an essential part of architectural heritage here. But in some cases new canopies have been fitted: at 1090 Homer Street this has been done with chunky modern steelwork, not unsympathetic to the 1910 building, as part of a renovation by Novam Development, who have established a reputation for this type of warehouse conversion.

One of the most recent heritage issues in Vancouver is the fate of the Stanley Theatre on South Granville Street. In 1991 Famous Players closed the cinema, a South Granville landmark for sixty years, despite a feisty campaign to keep it open. Thousands of people signed petitions in a protest which went all the way to Vancouver City Hall.

The Stanley was built in 1931 by architects McCarter & Nairne for proprietor Frederick Guest. The Moorish facade is a touch of Casablanca on South Granville, and inside there's an equally escapist auditorium domed in Italianate style. On the street, the 1940s marquee with its neon and bold typography adds a period flavour to the design. This feature alone is worth preserving, even though it's not the original. One of the thrills of an early evening drive into the city was to see the Stanley's marquee illuminated against the backdrop of the city centre and the North Shore mountains beyond.

Largely unaltered, the Stanley is still a gem of 1930s cinema architecture. It is difficult to imagine its special aura surviving conversion no matter how cleverly and sensitively that is done. How many of the design features that give the Stanley its character would be retained? What meaning will they have even if they are? This is the challenge posed for heritage preservation where change of use is concerned. Some buildings can be adapted quite well, but not all and not always.

Famous Players might have been expected to appreciate the Stanley—they had owned it since 1941, the heyday of the Hollywood studio system. And City Council members might have been expected to support preservation—but they seemed to view the closure not as an opportunity for the city to negotiate for the survival and future use of a cultural asset, but as yet another irritating heritage issue. City planners say they intend to make any developer who buys the Stanley retain the building. With this constraint and Famous Players' desire to prevent any future owner from showing films in it, the cinema could remain derelict for years to come. Various deals have fallen through since it was closed, including conversion to a shopping mall. More hopeful was a proposal involving stage performance. But even if the building is eventually saved, its special meaning as Vancouver's best-preserved 1930s picture palace will not survive the radical change of use a developer would require. Every aspect of the Stanley's architectural and cultural character is tied to its use as a cinema or to some related function.

In a city that hosts major film and jazz festivals, and where arts and community organizations are crying out for exhibiting and performing space, City Council's blinkered attitude on this issue continues to be thoroughly depressing. So too their reluctance to invest public money to ensure the survival of such a potentially useful community facility. Vancouver Council could have negotiated a density transfer or land swap with Famous Players in order to take over the Stanley, refurbish it and run it as a publicly funded arts centre, cinema and theatre or library if there had been the foresight and political will to do so.

The Coliseum Theatre at the corner of Third Avenue and
Pike Street was built in 1916 and is one of the grandest theatres in North America specifically designed for motion pic-
tures (music halls, whose gilded decor picture palaces
copied, had previously been adapted for film).

Architect Benjamin Marcus Priteca studied in Europe
and, when he returned to America, went to work with Alexander Pantages, the Greek waiter and impresario who
began his theatrical career in the Klondike gold fields.
Priteca applied his knowledge of Beaux Arts design to terra-
cotta, a cheap but durable substitute for stone, which could
be used to mass-produce the classical columns, cartouches
and other architectural embellishments that dignified commercial buildings and lent exotic fantasy to the theatres of
the time.

The Coliseum is clad with a spectacular veneer of glazed
white terra-cotta typography, festoons, friezes, cartouches,
garlands of fruit and foliage and Minoan bullock heads—
all of classical inspiration, and all topped with an elaborate
neoclassical cornice. The building's tour de force is the
bold, concave corner. This quite stunning use of space de-
fines the entrance to an auditorium, now past its prime,
which once twinkled with lights like twilight stars. Outside,
a domed Beaux Arts marquee once filled the corner but
was replaced by an odd 1950s period piece. The Coliseum
is currently semi-derelict but proposals for retail use should
see the exterior, at least, restored to its former grandeur.
Unlike Vancouver's Stanley Theatre, the Coliseum is a
huge building and so overdecorated that its presence is unlikely to be diminished by change of use.

The Orpheum Theatre at 884 Granville Street in Vancouver is a special place, not least because it was one of the city's earliest and most successful heritage conservation efforts. Popular demand and civic pride saved the theatre in 1973 when it was threatened with demolition. The auditorium was restored in 1975, and the stage rebuilt with a backdrop echo of the 1927 original's flamboyant, picture palace Renaissance style.

Unfortunately, the Hollywood-cum-music hall historicism inside was not carried through to the Smithe Street elevation during restoration. There, a foyer extension and new entrance work spatially, but turn in a lacklustre performance compared to the wonderous 1927 interior. What the Smithe Street exterior needed was an elevation with the panache of Seattle's Coliseum — an entrance that would have given a true sense of occasion to one's entry into this extraordinary theatre: a lusty overture of Beaux Arts postmodernism reworking the burlesque theatre architecture of the Edwardian era or the Hollywood fantasies of the 1920s, or perhaps monumental, concrete modernism — and a theatrical marquee and a neon sign. But neither the Smithe Street entrance nor the gigantic old sign and miniature Beaux Arts facade on Granville Street prepare you for the wonders of the Orpheum's interior. Perhaps this is just as well — the auditorium comes as even more of a surprise. I was advised to take a large sketchbook with me. My informant was not wrong.

The original foyer is a galleried hall styled in baronial Spanish Renaissance. But even this space, with its paired colonettes, pseudo-Gothic details, Moorish arches and coffered ceiling, is overwhelmed by the auditorium's spectacular decor. The American architect Benjamin Marcus Priteca employed a wild melange of exotic architectural detail — a cantata of columns, cartouches and chandeliers — to embellish the auditorium, living up to his reputation as the doyen of West Coast theatre designers. He designed over sixty theatres up and down the west coast from Alaska to San Diego during his fifty-year career, begun in 1910. Priteca's signature both outside and in his buildings was romantic with florid, gilded architectural fantasy, as far-fetched as anything projected on the silver screen, which would keep patrons suitably agog while they awaited a performance, creating the perfect mood for the moment when the house lights dimmed.

*   *   *